WHERE ARE YOU FROM?

Where I'm from doesn't matter,
Nor, where I am going,
For, right here, right now,

This is home as I like to call it.

-Neal

Copyright © 2020 by Neal Eisler

All rights reserved. Printed in the United States of America. No part of this book may be reproduced, distributed, or transmitted in any form or by any means, including photocopying, recording, or other electronic or mechanical methods, without the prior written permission of the author, Neal Eisler. Except in the case of brief quotations embodied in critical articles and reviews. For more information, address: NealTheEarthling@gmail.com.

FIRST EDITION

Book Design by Lyn Sweet
Poetry by Neal Eisler

Library of Congress Cataloging-in-Publication Data

Library of Congress Control Number: 2020942041

ISBN 978-1-7353554-0-5 (paperback)
ISBN 978-1-7353554-1-2 (eBook)

Published by *Dream World Publishing*™
Oak View, CA

www.NealTheEarthling.com
@NealTheEarthling

WHERE ARE YOU FROM?

WRITTEN BY NEAL THE EARTHLING
ILLUSTRATED BY LYN THE ALIEN

PROLOGUE
CHILDHOOD TRAUMA

Childhood trauma
Filled with drama.

Haunted,
Sad,
Mad;
The opposite of rad.

No one to listen;
No one to hear.
Lost in fear;
Stuck in low gear.

A victim of the past;
It continues to last.

Childhood trauma
Causing drama.

Reflections,
Deflections,
Fractured sections.

Of my mind;
Out of kind.
Unwilling to find;
This is the crime.

A victim of the past;
It continues to last.
Moving so fast;
History cast.

Childhood trauma;
All the drama.
Unable to sleep;
Insomnia seeps.

Understand,
This was not planned.
Trauma fanned,
Bottled and canned.

Please hear,
'This is my fear.'
I wanna share,
'Don't you care?'

'Does anyone care?'

Blank stares,
Nobody cares.
Looking in the rear
To see an evil glare.

A victim of the past;

My
childhood
trauma
will
always
last.

SENSITIVE CREATURE

It's made me a sensitive creature.

A sensitive creature,
Each and every feature.
This sensitive creature;
A screecher.

Don't touch me;
Don't look at me;
Don't hear me.

I'm a sensitive creature.

Don't feel me;
Don't watch me;
Don't listen to me.

I'm a sensitive creature.

Don't hold me;
Don't see me;
Don't understand me.

I'm a sensitive creature!

I'm a sensitive creature;
A sensitive creature,
Each and every feature.

This sensitive creature,
No longer a screecher.
Now, I'm a preacher.

Hear me;
Look at me,
Touch me.

Listen to me;
Watch me,
Feel me.

Understand me;
See me,
Hold me.

Never let go;
Never let me go.

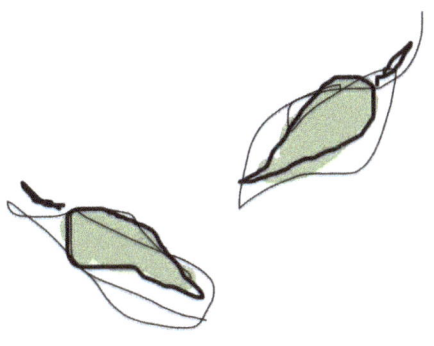

I'm a sensitive creature;
A sensitive creature.

Sensitive creature.

Searching for a home
To call my own.
Where I can express what life has shown?
Through each one of these poems.

SEARCHING FOR HOME

Earth: A planet,
In the Milky Way;
An earthling found his way.
Searching for home—
One not yet known.

Beyond this Galaxy—
Infiniti, maybe.
Life, rife with possibility.

But, the likely probability;
This earthling would never
Ever reach full potential,
Which is exponential.

Being one amongst the stars.

Trying to gain stability;
Immense capability;
Overcome by ineffability.

I want to be able...

Able to perceive;
Able to believe;
Able to receive.

I want to be able to find my truth.
Stop the lies
And defy;
Society's cries.

Before death,
What would it mean to take a full breath?

Inhaling; exhaling.
Letting everything go.

Beneath stars;
Free of wars.
Settling old scores;
Walking through new doors.

Within an ever-expanding universe,
Are we cursed?

A light burst!

WHERE AM I?

Signal blocked;
Receiver knocked.

Turning back the clock.

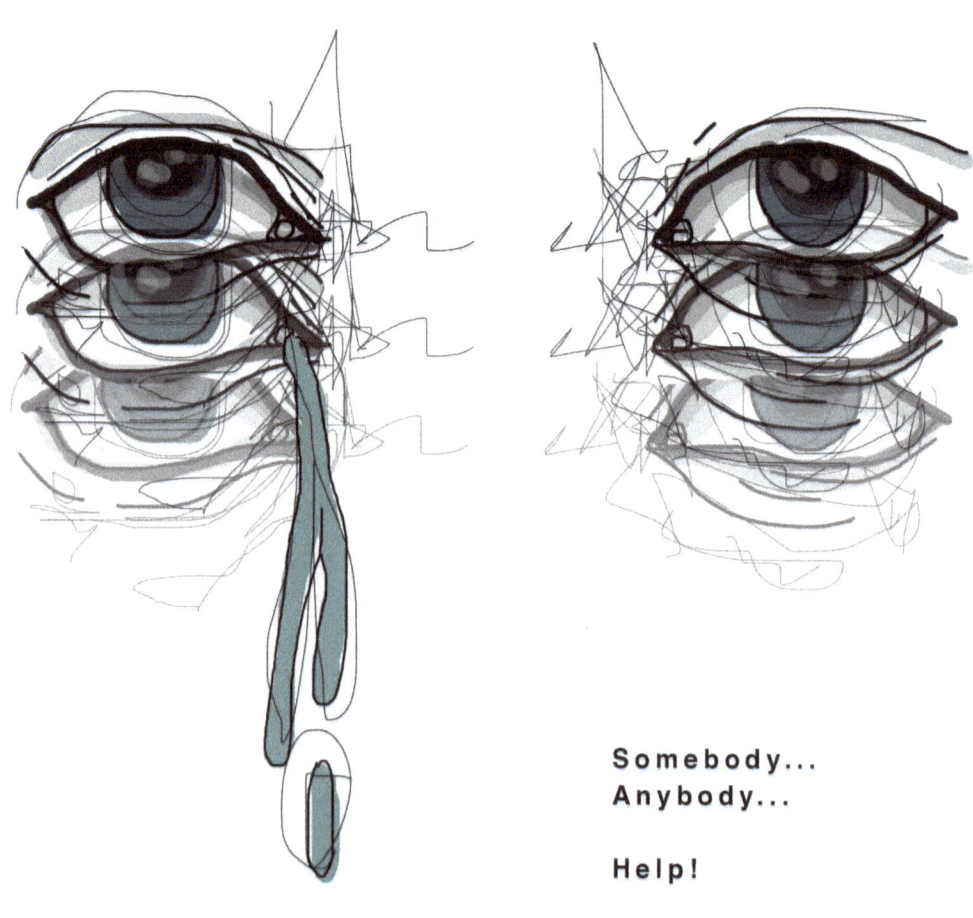

Are we unique?
What is it we seek?
My body starts to leak;
Unable to speak.

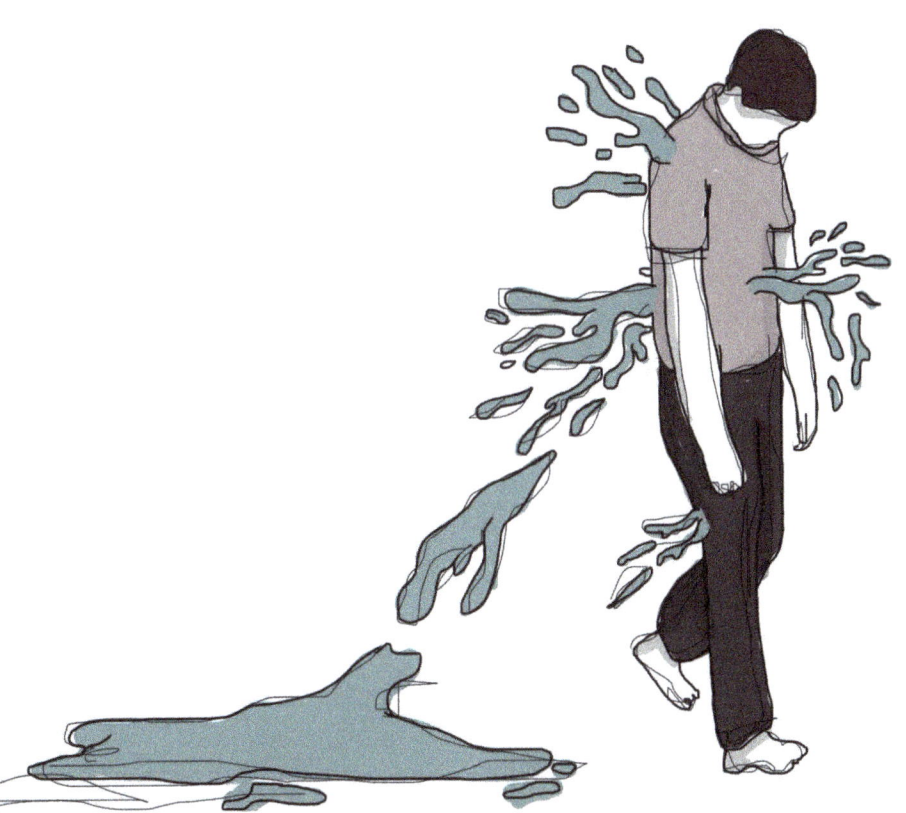

Alien clone?
'Alien clone?'

Am I a clone?!

I talk like a drone,

I moan and I moan.
All alone;
Searching for home.

Am I a clone?...
An alien clone?

Is this home?

Where is home?

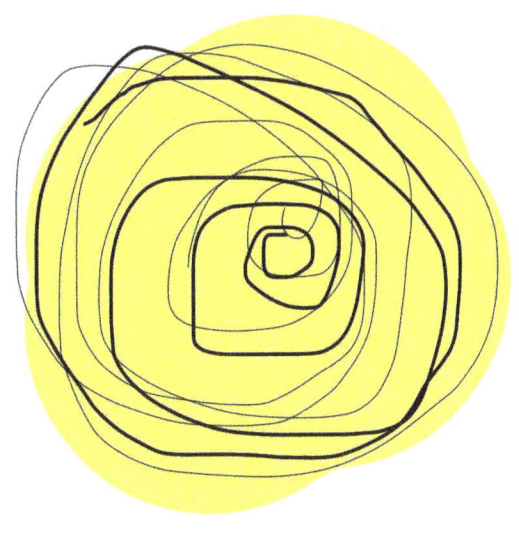

'Where is home?'

Where is home?
It is unknown.

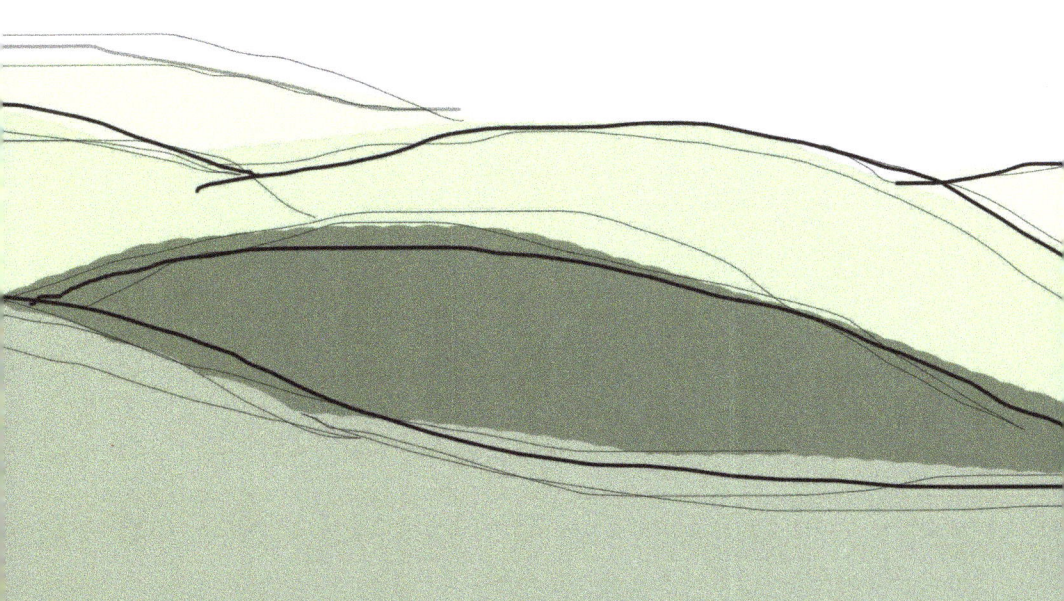

WHERE AM I FROM?

Where am I from?
Under the sun
Never having fun,
Life unbegun.

I was lost; at a loss,
Stuck under an albatross.

Calling out; all about,
Nobody heard my shout;
Or, my silent bout.

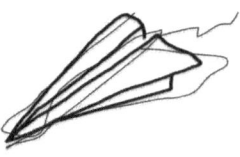

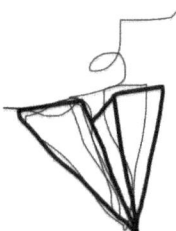

Searching sea, please see, me,
Me,
Me...

Me!

Find me; truly;
Let me be.

Hear me;
Save me;
Believe in my humanity.

Humanity,
Calamity;
Deformity,
Conformity.

Feeling indifference,
To our difference.

You must fit in;
You must sit in;
Until you begin
To forget where you've been.

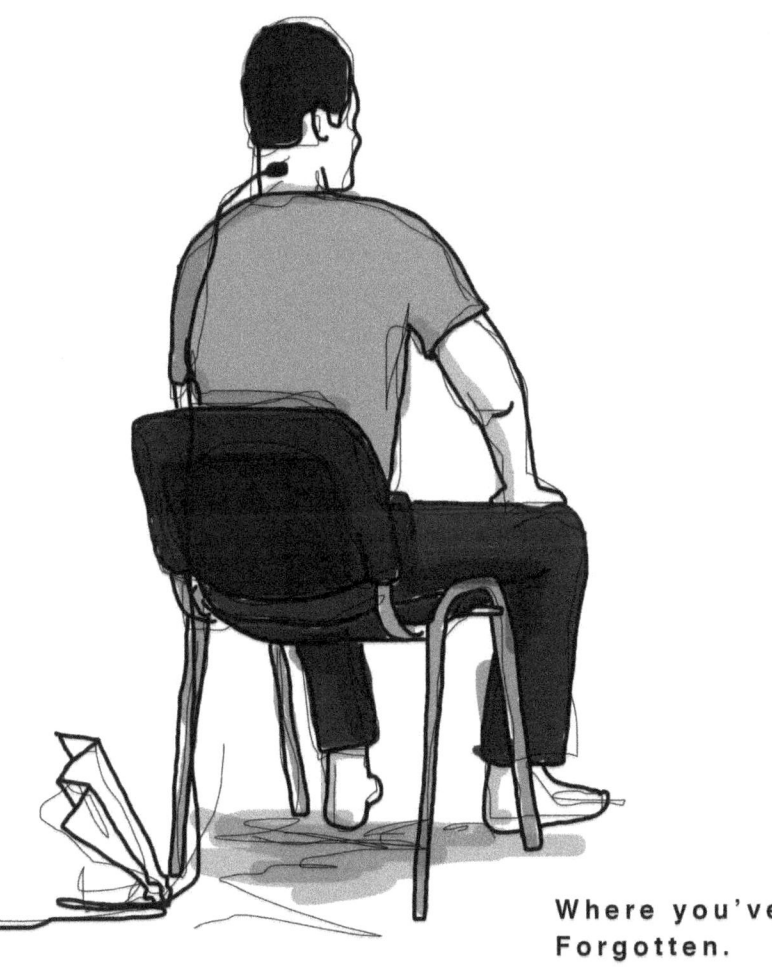

Where you've been-
Forgotten.

You've been forgotten.

You've been forgotten.

You've been forgotten.

Goodbye.

Everything goes black.

WHERE DID EVERYONE GO?

Where did everyone go?
Nowhere I know.

No goodbyes,
Just byes.

Here I sigh,
And I cry,
As I try,
To stop being so shy.

They called me a snitch,
They told me I make them itch,
You've got a weird pitch!

So, they ditched me,
they ditched me...

they ditched me.

Here I sigh
And I cry
As I try
To stop being so shy.

Feeling left out;
Lost about.

Alone;
Alone.
Shivers to the bone
Feeling blown,
All alone.

All alone, like an alien clone.

I must be a clone-
An alien clone;
My life has shown.

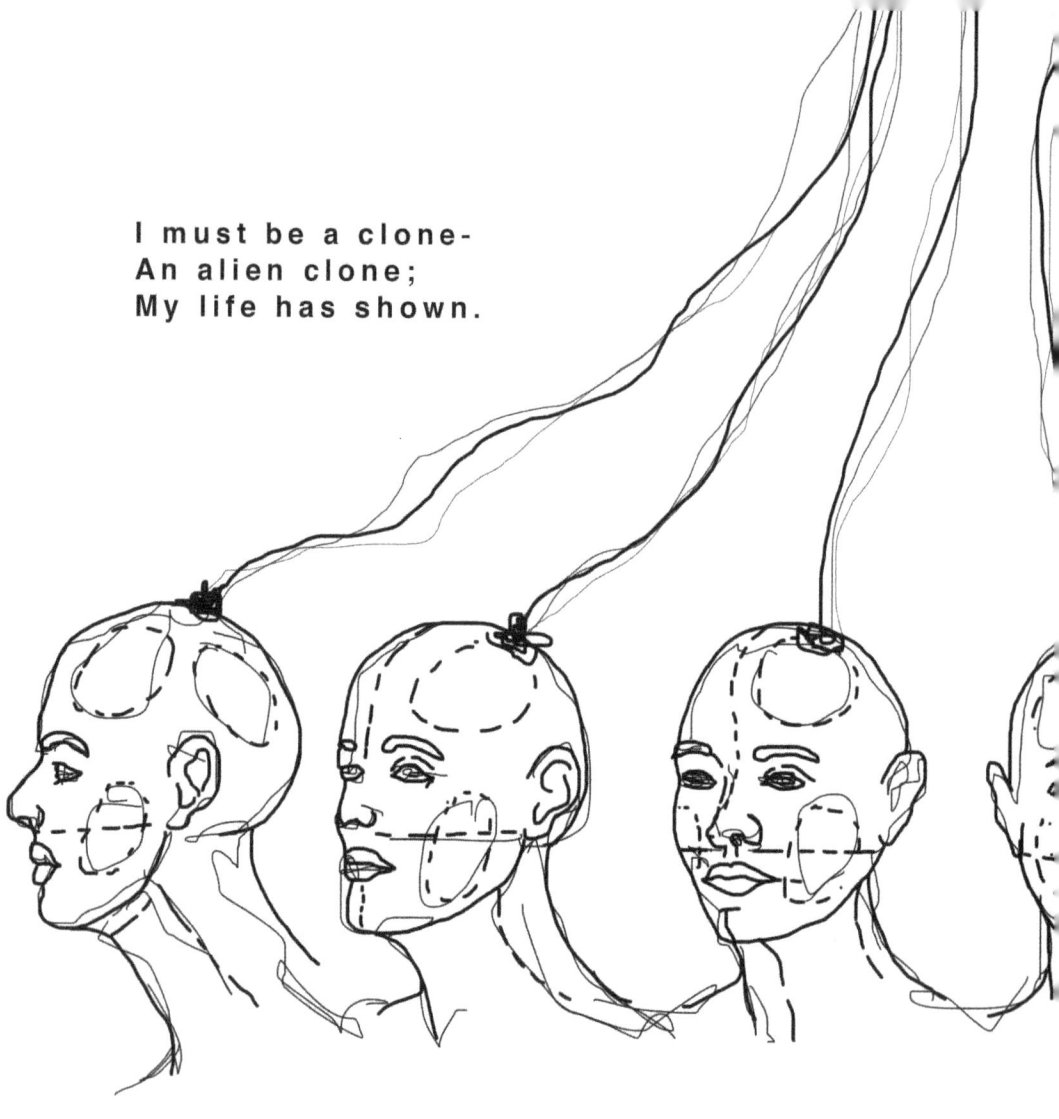

Until wishing upon a star,
From afar.

For a new home,
An alien stone;
Becoming this Earthlings own.

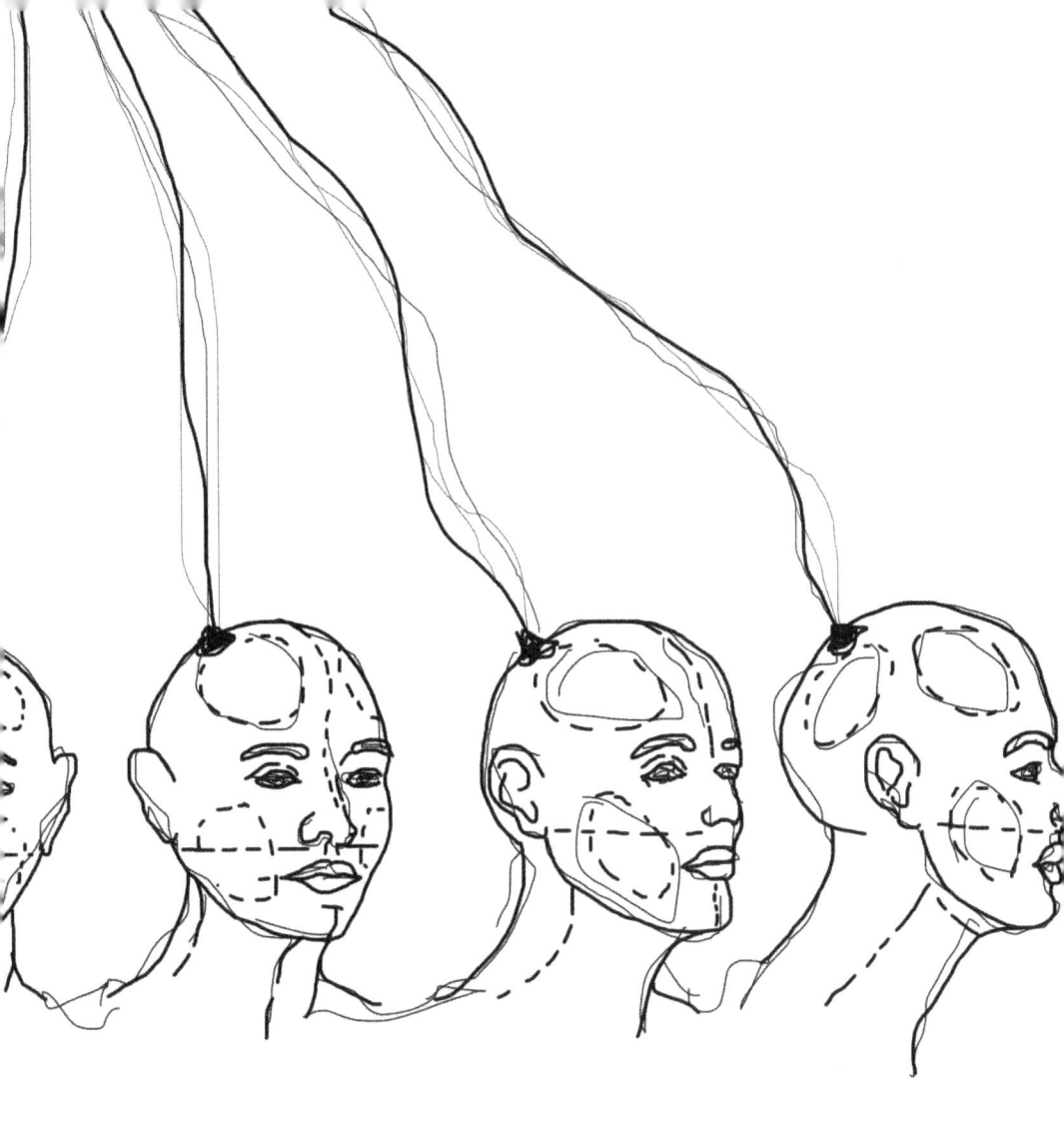

But, it's not yet known,
This alien's home.
Still unknown,..

To an alien clone.

AM I ALONE?

Am I alone?

Hello.

Hello!

My mind blown
Searching for home.
Continue to roam
Until I've grown.

Nothing known
Nothing shown.

Am I alone?
An alien clone?
With no home?

Hello?

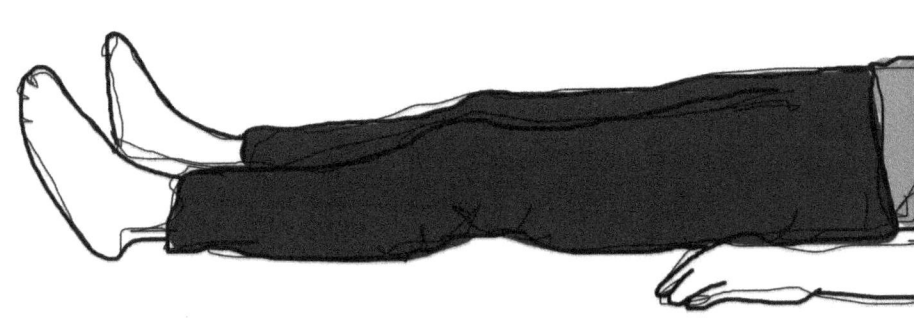

How can my mind,..
What can I find?

Please, don't remind, me,
Please don't,
I won't; I won't!.

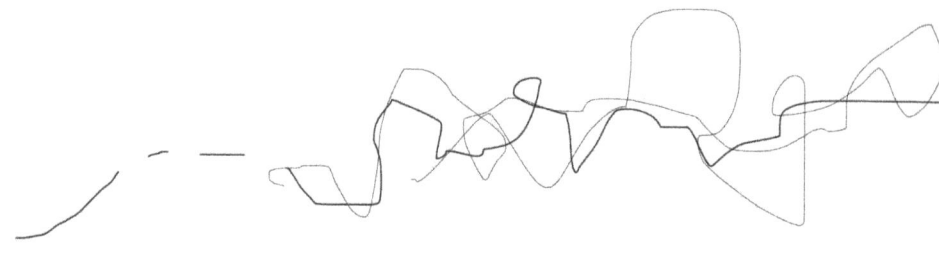

All alone; all alone.
Shivers to the bone;
Nothing is known.
Nothing is shown;
Mind is blown
Like a drone.

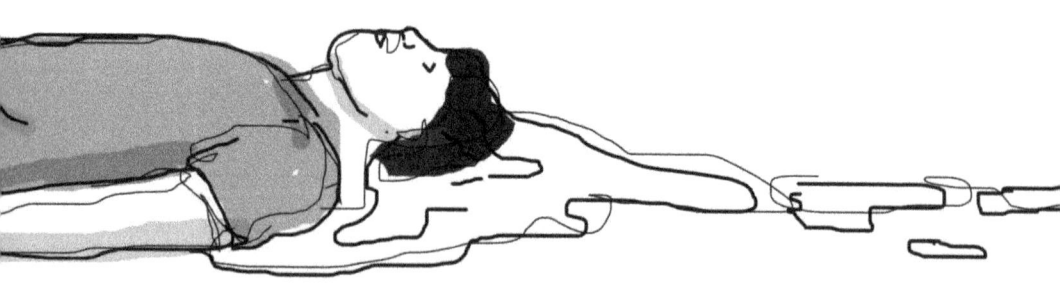

Alone, alone,
Do you hear my moan?
Do you hear my groan?
My silent tone?

'Am I alone?'

I must be.

IS THIS HOME?

All alone;
Until I find home;
What life has shown;
I'm not homegrown.

Home, home,
Never known.

Never known...

Until I roam,
Through white foam; of,

Waterfalls,
   River rapids,
      Ocean waves
         Watery
            graves,

The path it paves;
Oh, how it saves...

Freed from being slaves.

From land to sea;
What you will see?
Might not agree;
Though will answer your plea.

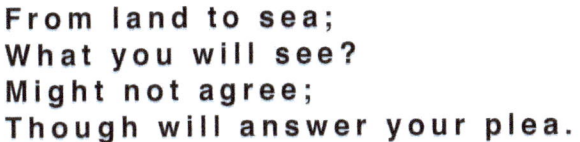

      Searching,
          Scorching,
              Sunlit rays,

    New ways,
    Each one of these days.

Not yet known, my home,
What life has shown;
I'm not home grown.

        Where is home,
        In this vast unknown;
        Where is home?

Let me grab my alien phone.

This Earthling's mind still blown.
Lost and alone;
Searching for a home,
Not yet known.

HOW DO YOU FEEL?

How do you feel,
Is this real?

In a field,
Under a shield,
We plan to build
Will it yield?

Seeds planted;
Lives granted.

Time grown;
Vortex sewn,

Nothing to own
But what's been blown.

Uprooted,

Looted,

Muted

Silence speaks,

Nothing leaks,

Only squeaks

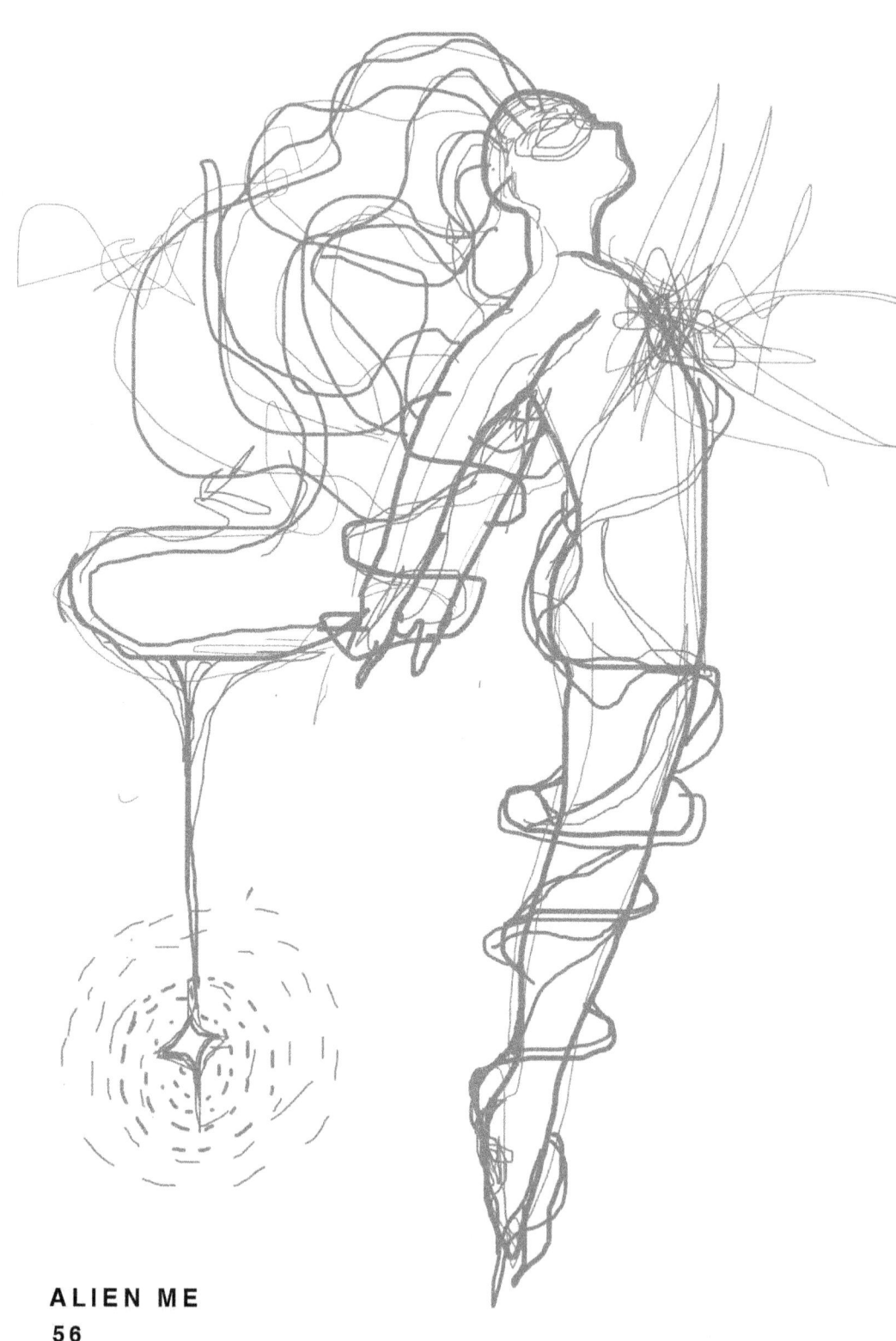

ALIEN ME

Abducted,
Conducted,
Reconstructed.

Listen here,
Go there,
Not there,
You have to care.

Mind swapped,
No opt;
Out, about to be...

Told what to see
Taught by decree.
Nowhere to flee
One way to be.

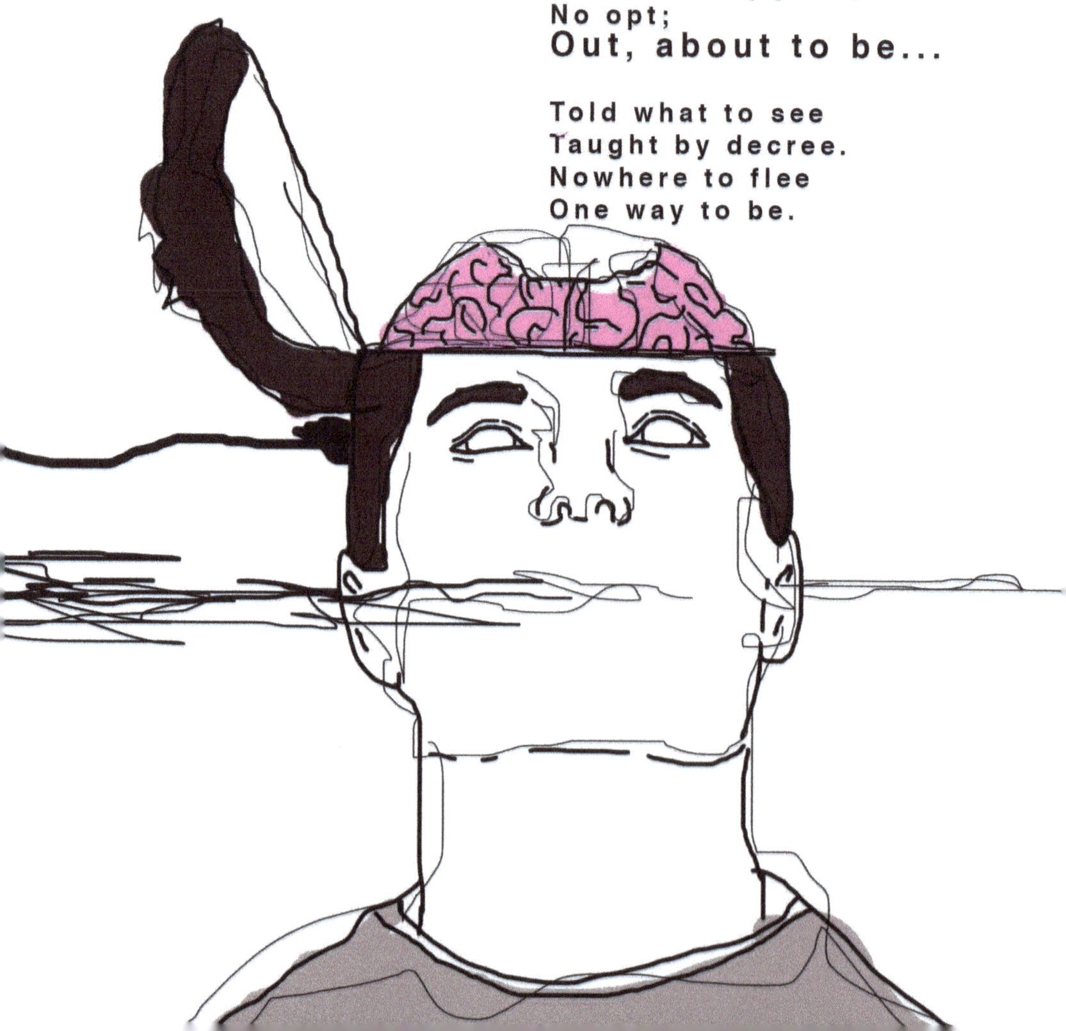

Alien me.

Not yet free;
I'm alien to me.

Alien me.

NEVER FREE

A flash!

Flash!
'Flash!'

Foreign as can be
All anyone could see
Was alien me.

Stuck in cage
Feeling the rage
Unable to turn a page.

I was drowning in the sea;
My only key was to be;
Alien free.

But, it couldn't be;
I was alien me.

Water overwhelmed
Encompassing the helm.

Getting sucked in
Trying to swim.

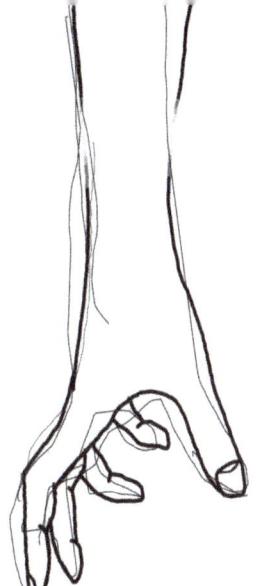

Uhhhhhhh...

Ahhhhhhhh....

Uhhhhhaaahhhhhh....

DROWNING IN THE SEA

Air bubbles
Toxic troubles
Seeing doubles.

Looking up
At what was once below.
Nothing glows;
Everything slows.

Water shimmers;
Sunshine glimmers.
Hope simmers;
Eyes become dimmers.

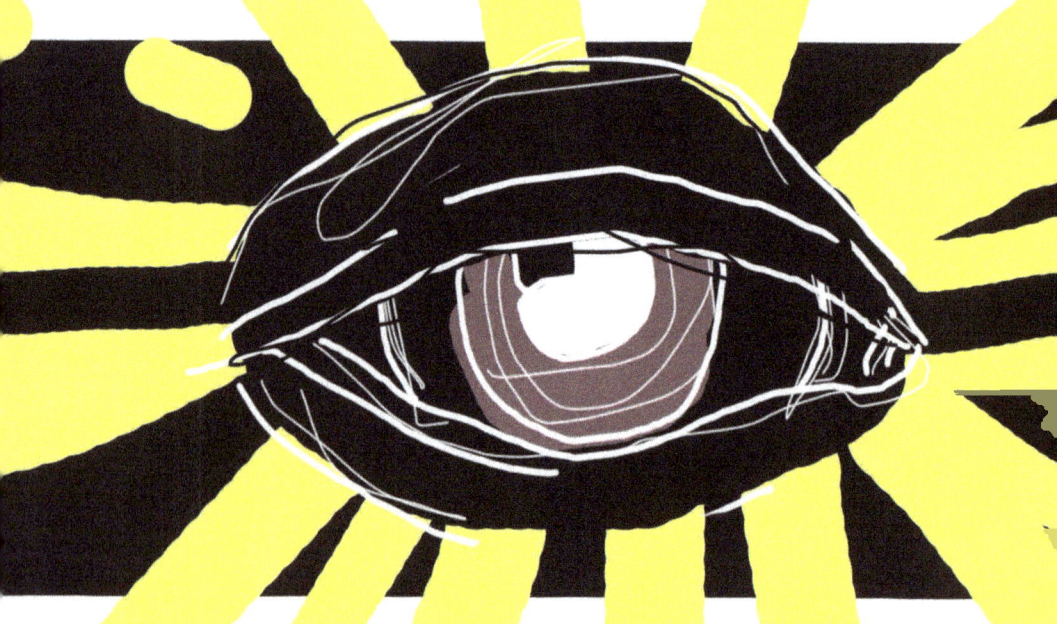

Closing lids
To our inner kids
Overtaken by squids.

All I could see
Was alien me-
Foreign as can be.

Alien me-
Foreign as can be.

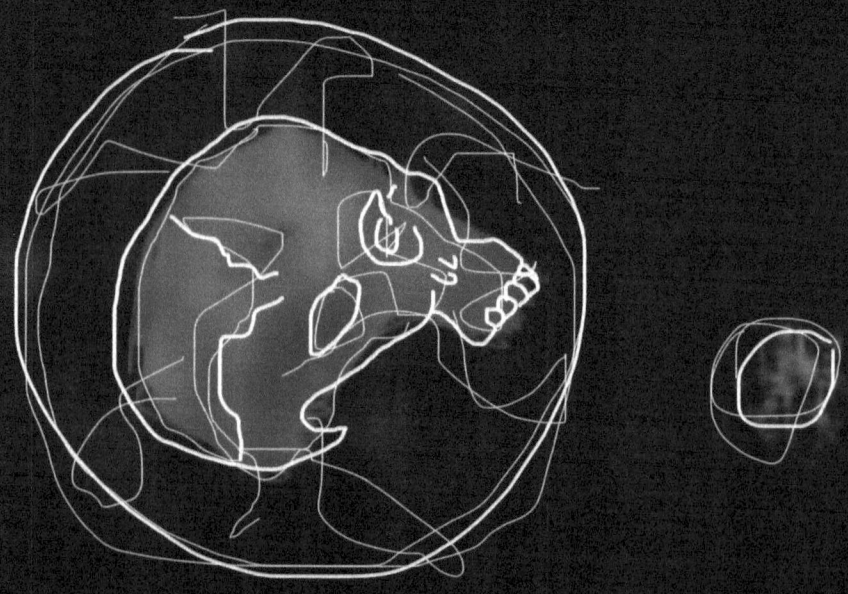

STILL SEARCHING FOR HOME

Still searching for home;
Shivers to the bone.

Rhythmic sound;
Arithmetic bound.
Mind wound
All around.

The world goes around.
Round and round;
What's there to be found?

                                        Alien clones?
                                        We are all alone.

We talk like drones;
We moan and we moan.

Searching for purpose;
Slower than a tortoise.

What's the rush?
Painting a world with a brush.

With just the right touch,
Not too much,
Such and such;
Letting go of any crutch.

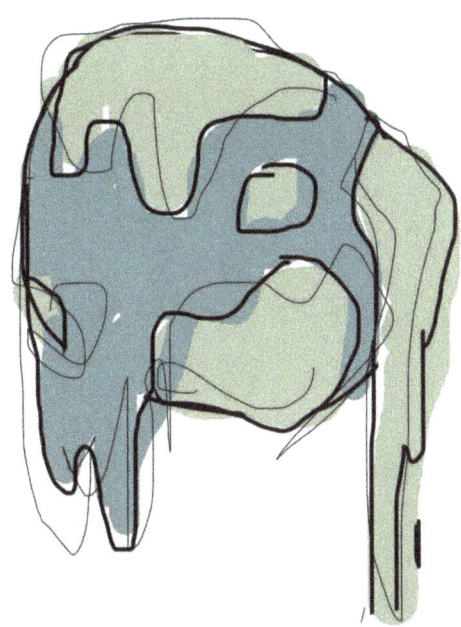

Chords strike our bones;
Minds become known.

What life has shown
Is that we are not alone.
Alien clones
Or drones.

Once unknown;
Mystery blown.

One universe;
One simple verse.

Rhythmic sound;
Arithmetic unbound.

Earthling found
Being crowned.
From afar
Here you are.

Just another simple star.

You are not alone;
An alien clone
Or a drone.
Life has shown.

Life has shown you;
Where is home?

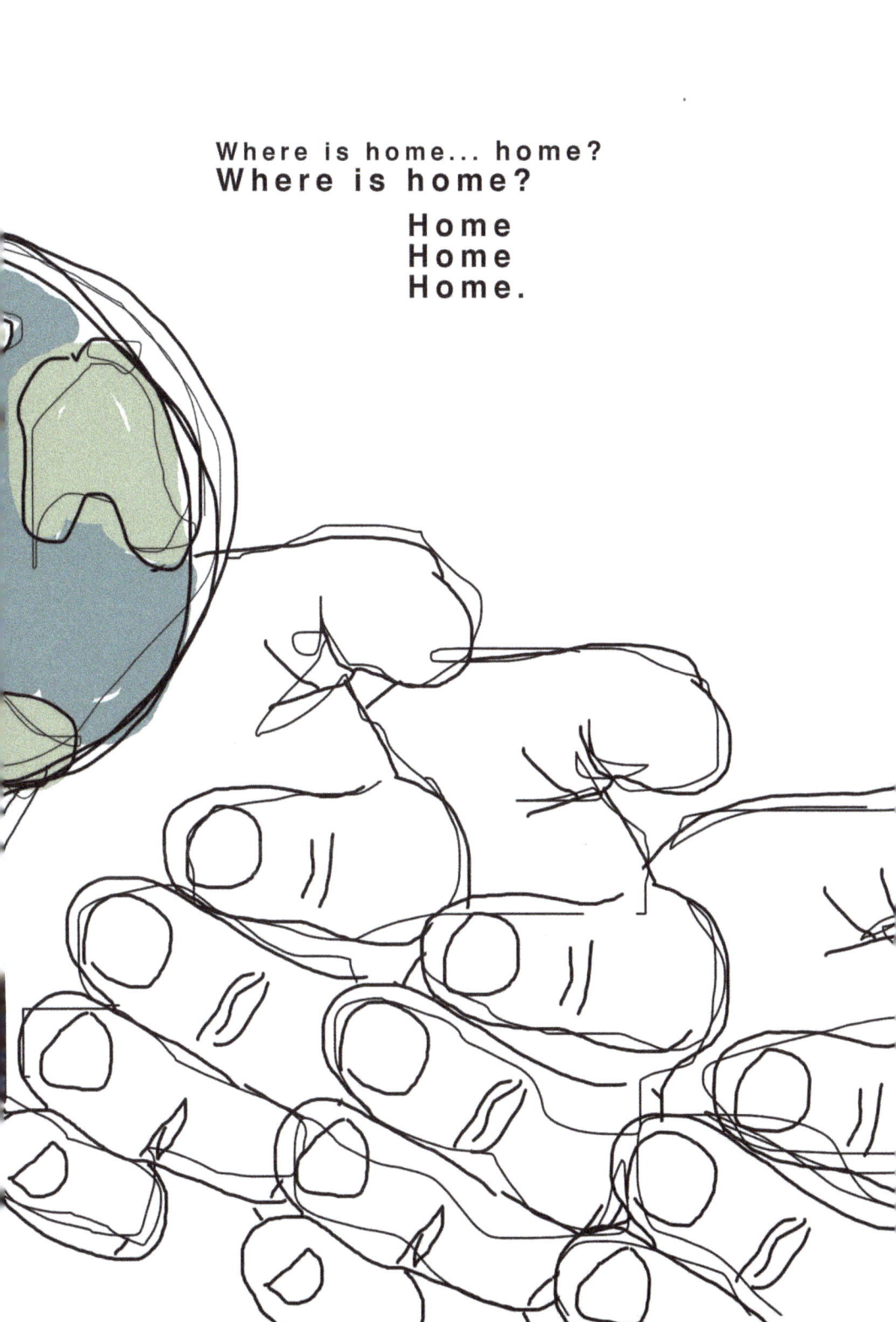

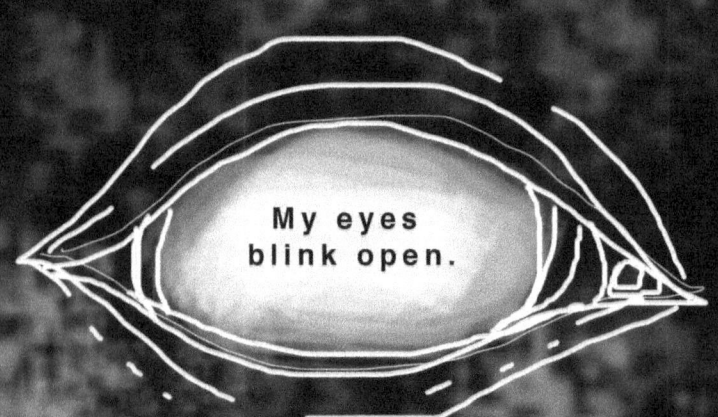

Just another scene from the same dream.
So it seems... so it seems.

We are always searching for home.
Lost in this world all alone.

MY PURPOSE KNOWN

My purpose known
To find home
Until I'm not alone;
The real unknown.

Evil as can be;
All eyes can see.

Fighting
Lighting
Burning
Yearning.

Warring factions cause inactions.

Infractions bring fractions.

Forgetful of our past;
How long will it last?

Evil as can be;
All eyes can see.

If hate will be our fate;
We are too late.

Purpose known
My own
To share this home
We call our own.

Choose love over fear
Give hate the stare;
Listen, hear,
Be aware...

Of this evil glare,
Some may share.

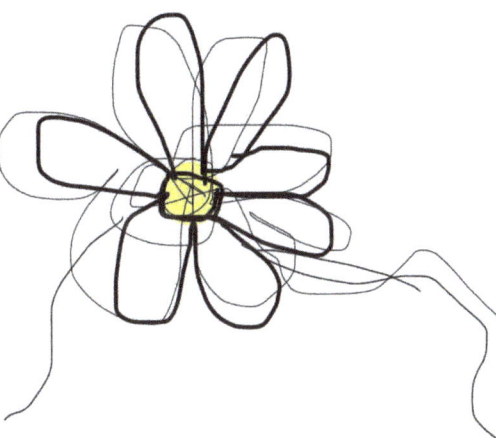

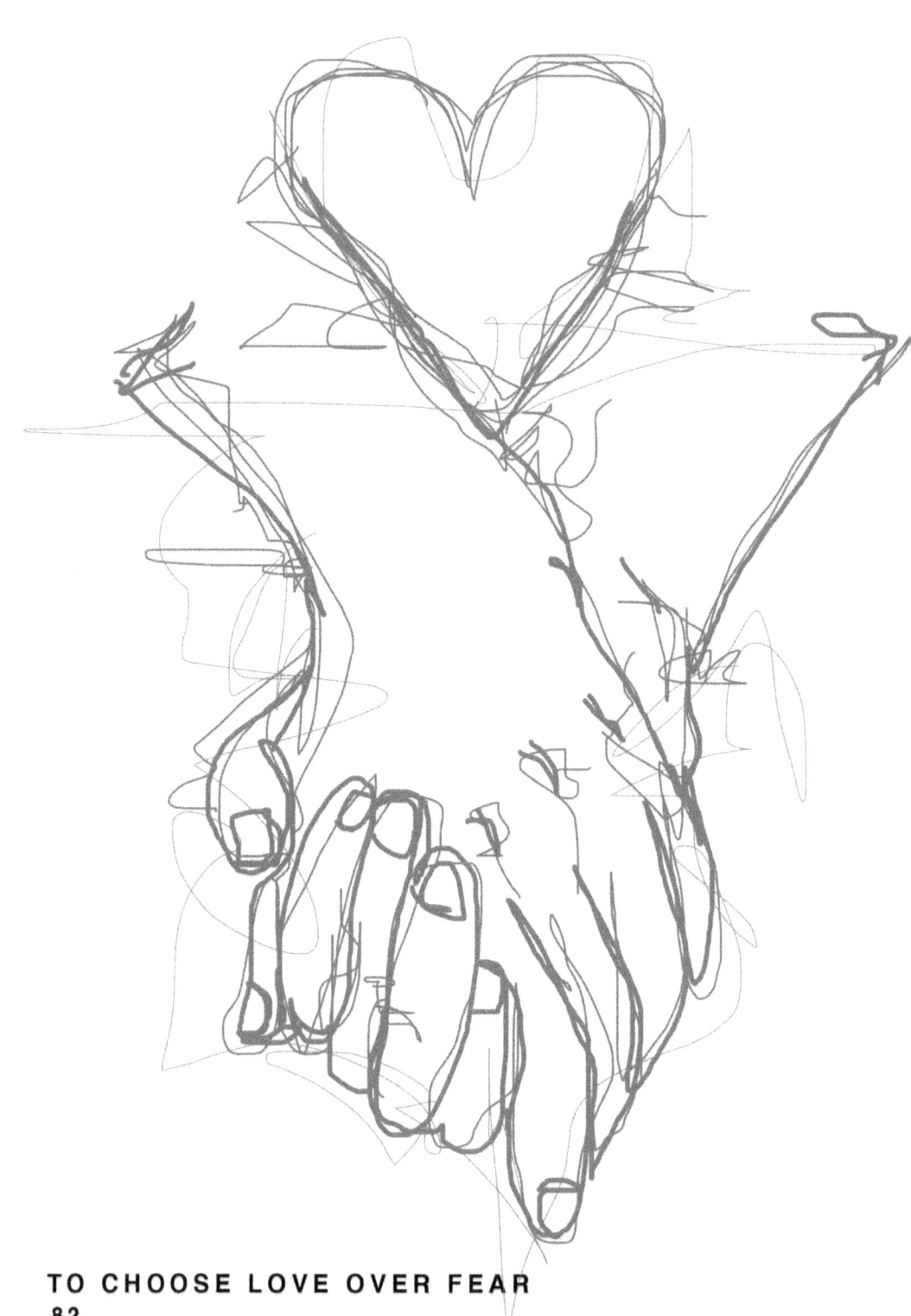

TO CHOOSE LOVE OVER FEAR

What we can share
Is very clear;
When we face fear
With love so bare.

Shadowlands
Stuck in sands;
Here fear stands
Life unplanned.

Choose love over fear
Give hate the stare;
Our love so rare
That we share.

Do you hear?
Do you care?
What it is I share?

This love I fear
Our tempers flare;
Quite a scare
This love we share.

Let your heart be bare
Open up here;
Fight the scare.

How we can,
How we can,
Change life's plan.

EVIL ACTS OF DESTRUCTION

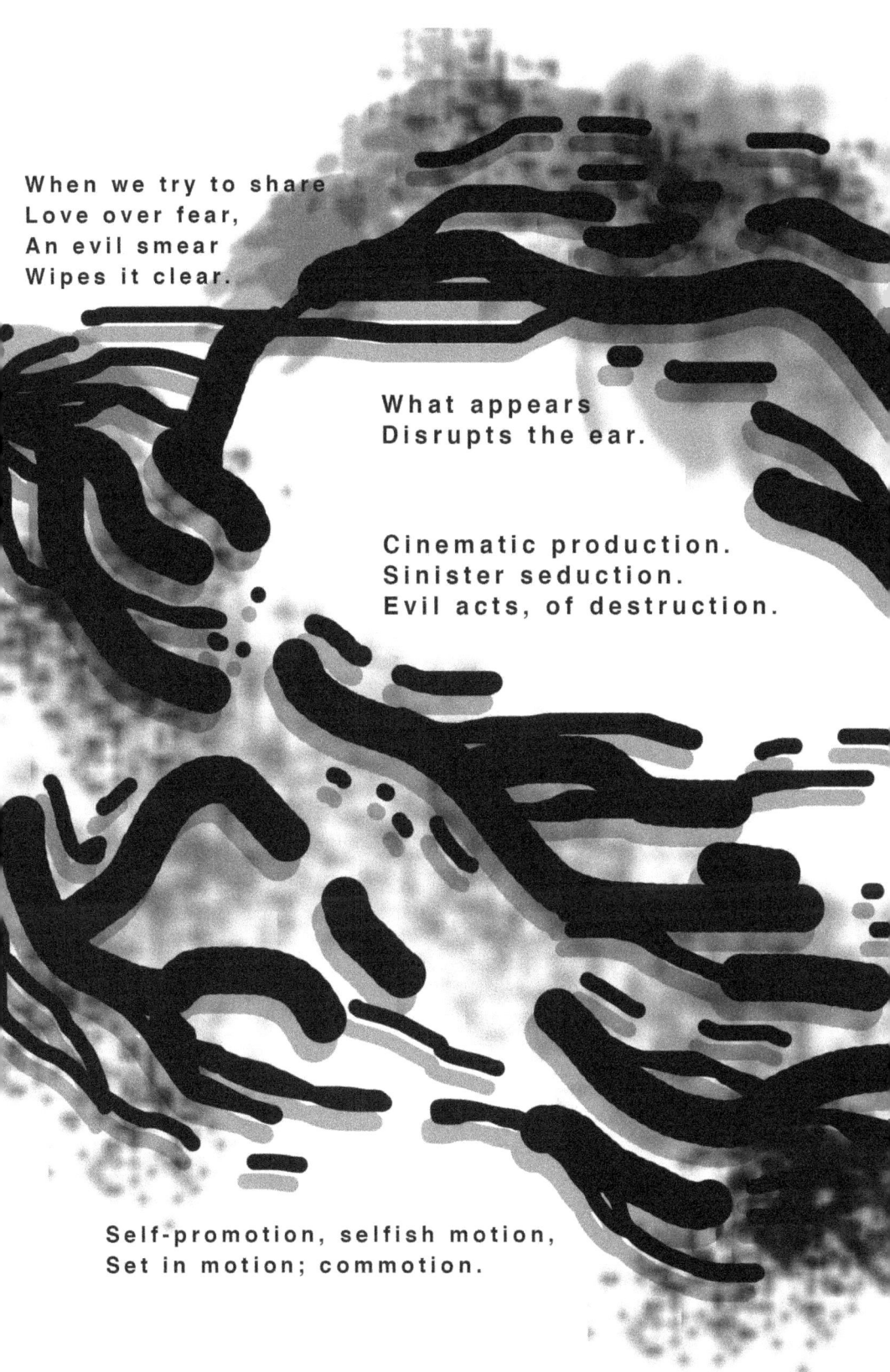

When we try to share
Love over fear,
An evil smear
Wipes it clear.

What appears
Disrupts the ear.

Cinematic production.
Sinister seduction.
Evil acts, of destruction.

Self-promotion, selfish motion,
Set in motion; commotion.

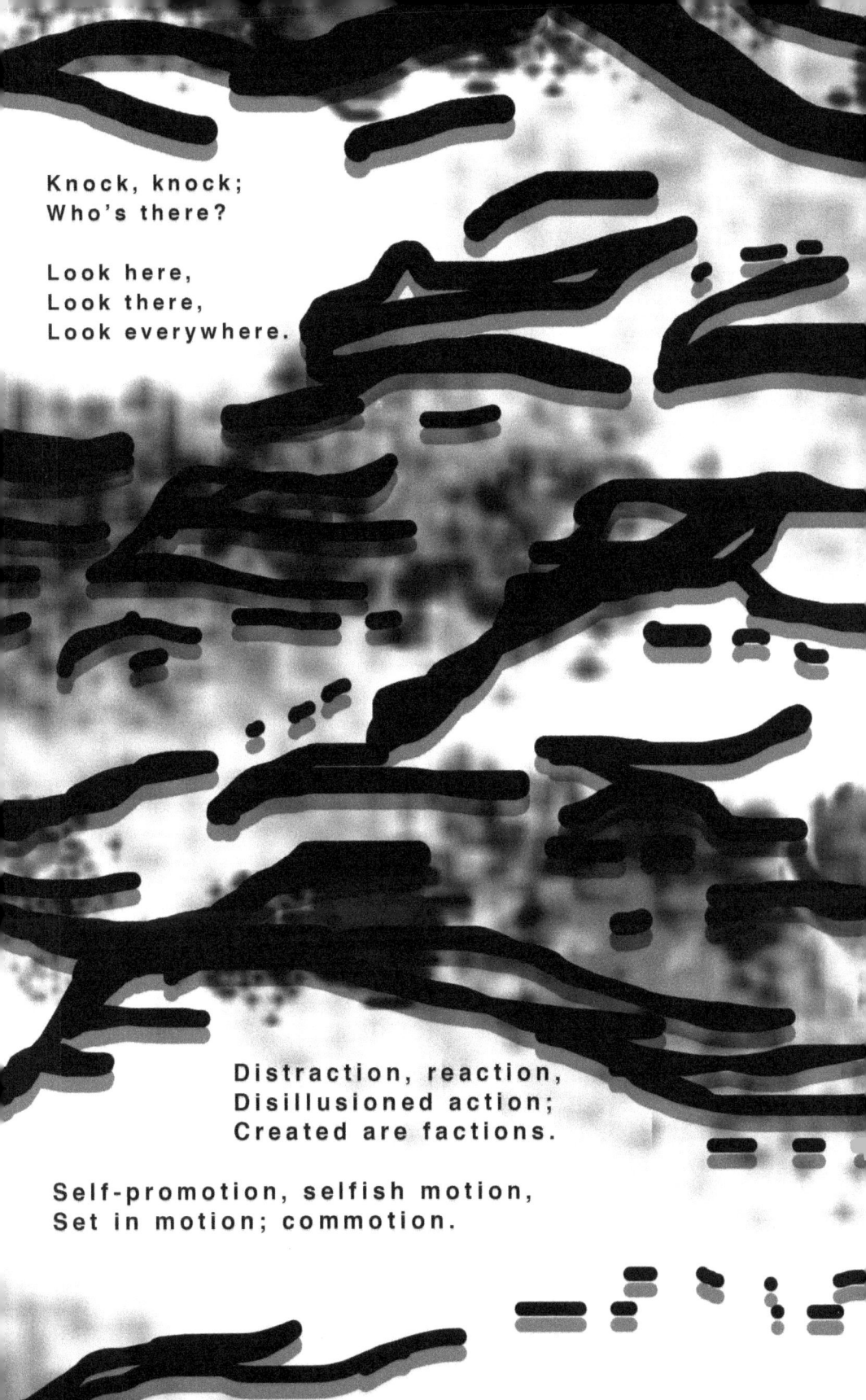

Knock, knock;
Who's there?

Look here,
Look there,
Look everywhere.

Distraction, reaction,
Disillusioned action;
Created are factions.

Self-promotion, selfish motion,
Set in motion; commotion.

Fearful emotion;
Hateful potion;
A flooding ocean.

Deception;
Inception;
A welcome reception.

Inflicting pain,
Right on aim;
Down comes the rain.

Self-promotion, selfish motion,
Set in motion; commotion.

Into storm drains
Sucked out brains;
Gone are flames
And our names.

Evil acts;
Evil acts
Facts.

Who needs facts
To commit evil acts.

'Maniacs!'

'Sociopaths!'

Evil acts
Evil acts.
No more facts
With evil acts.

With evil acts-
The world reacts.

The world reacts-
To evil acts.

THE WORLD REACTS

Positive energy attracts;
Like negative energy reacts.

Dulled senses
Building fences.

Dark matter
Black splatter,

Where is all the laughter?

Gravity pulls us in;
In that we swim.
Trapped within;
Fearful demons win.

Negativity drowns;
Sinking down, sinking down.
Sinking down to the ground;
Will we ever be found?

Inside a bubble
We continue to struggle.
Do not stop
Until it pops.

Arms reaching;
Voice screeching.
Over here!
Can't you hear?

Audible to nobody;
Silent tones, of life's moans.
One filled with groans.

All alone
Shivers to the bone.
The world reacts
To evil acts.

Boom!

An explosion;
Here comes an implosion.

Oh no...

'NOOOOOOOO!!!!'

Corrosion
Erosion
Life becomes frozen.

LIFE FREEZES

Life freezes
Everything seizes;
Our existence ceases.

Frozen in time
We cannot shine.
Do not whine
Or step out of line.

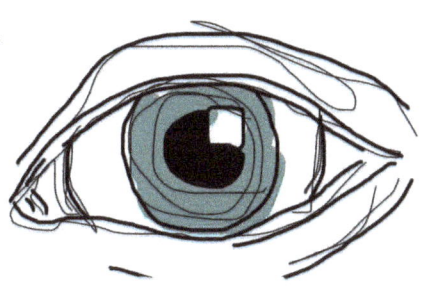

These uncertain facts
Make us feel attacked.
From a place of love, not fear;
Why can't anyone hear?

I want to share.
Please let me share.
Don't you care;
O' where o' where.

Where have you been, locked within.

Trained to be, trained to see;
Not trained to be free.

Programmed
Robotic.

Psychotic
Dichotic.

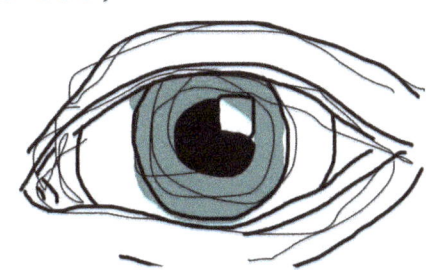

Does it scare you that I feel,
When I know your pain is real?

Let me help you heal,
Find your will;
A special deal.

Does it scare you that I feel,
When I know your pain is real?

Open up,
Express lost thoughts;
Pause to let them go.

Pause.

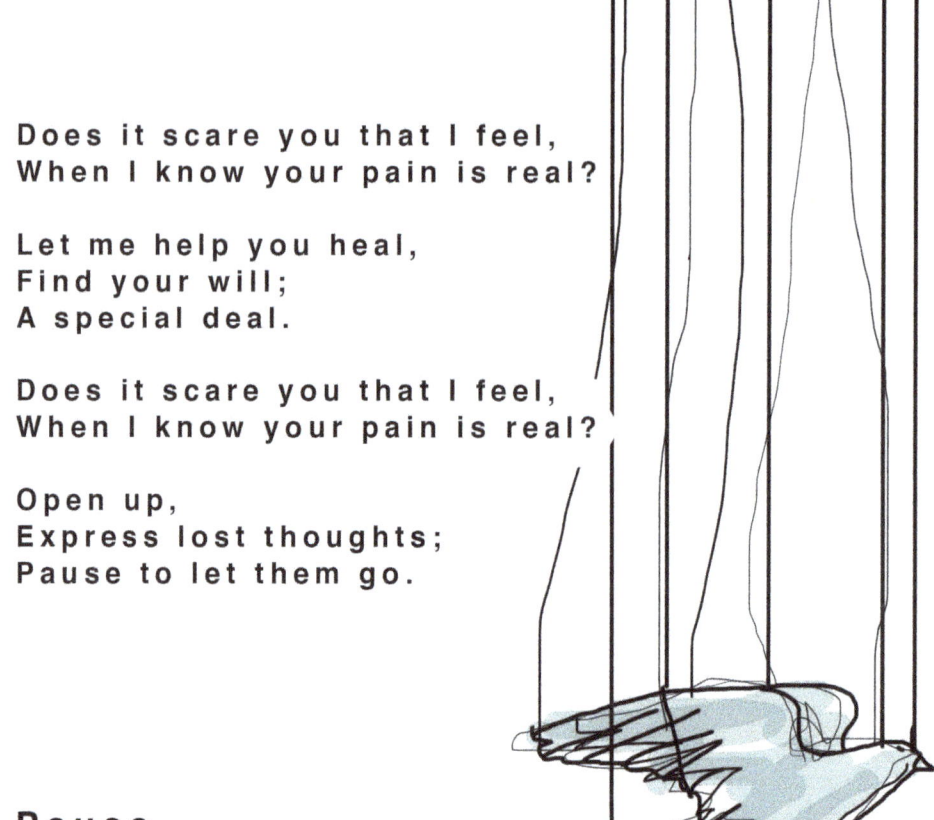

Breathing fire.

Huh huh huh huh huh huh huh

New tact;
Never looking back.
No need to react, I'm back on track.

Discovered, universal facts;
And my truth, that has always lacked.

AN ALIEN ACT

It was all an alien act;
Now I'm making a personal pact;
To regain the truth I've always lacked.

Here is where this alien sheds;
Free from fear
A mind becomes clear.

Out in the wilderness;
It's crazy, crazy;
Crazy beautiful out here.

Damn.

It's crazy to think about;
It's crazy to look back on things.

Damn, it's crazy.

Ha, haha, ha, ha, ha

I'm laughing because it's ridiculous.

That's as real as it gets.

I was doing it, the normal life.

What are we raised to do?

My parents;
They put me on a normal path.
I was pretty privileged.

No, I was really privileged.

It's crazy to think about
How many people don't understand;
They can't connect;
And, they have no perspective on life.

Hhhhhhhuhhhh.

I stop and I think;
God, I stop and I think about;
Where I was not too long ago.

I was in so much pain.
Mentally, physically, emotionally;
Understood by nobody.

An Alien.

An alien inside;
My earthling I did hide.

TO BE HONEST

I'm ready; to be honest.
Not just with myself;
But, with other people.

I've been holding back for quite a while;
That's the kind of mindset we get put in.

We stop thinking;
We stop realizing where we are going;
Because at the end of the day,
We are not going anywhere.

We stop expressing;
We stop listening to every being;
Because at the end of the day,
We are not being heard.

An impression with no expression.

Distractions
Creating factions.

Hard to focus;
Harder to see;
And yet, harder to be.

        To be free,
        To be me,
        Always and always.

        Society makes us feel like...
        Like, our path will be fulfilling;
        If only.

Instead we suffer.

We're not going anywhere

We are not home;
Our life has shown.

We are alone.

We are all alien clones.

Aliens,

Aliens.

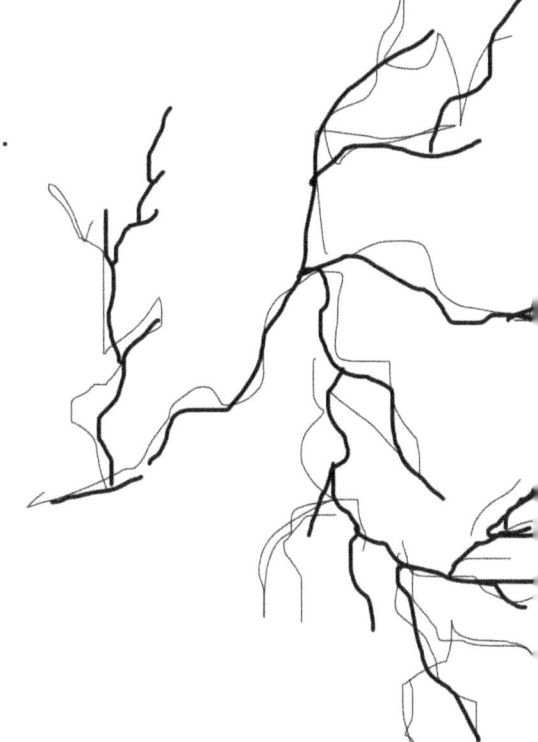

Until a light shows us home.

Crack!

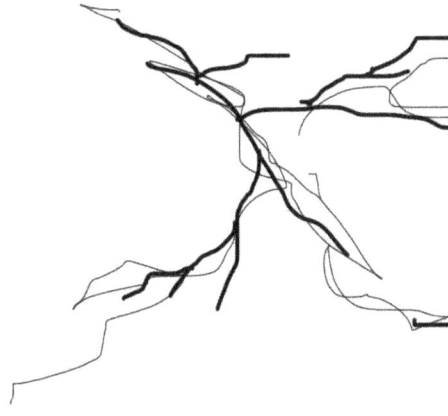

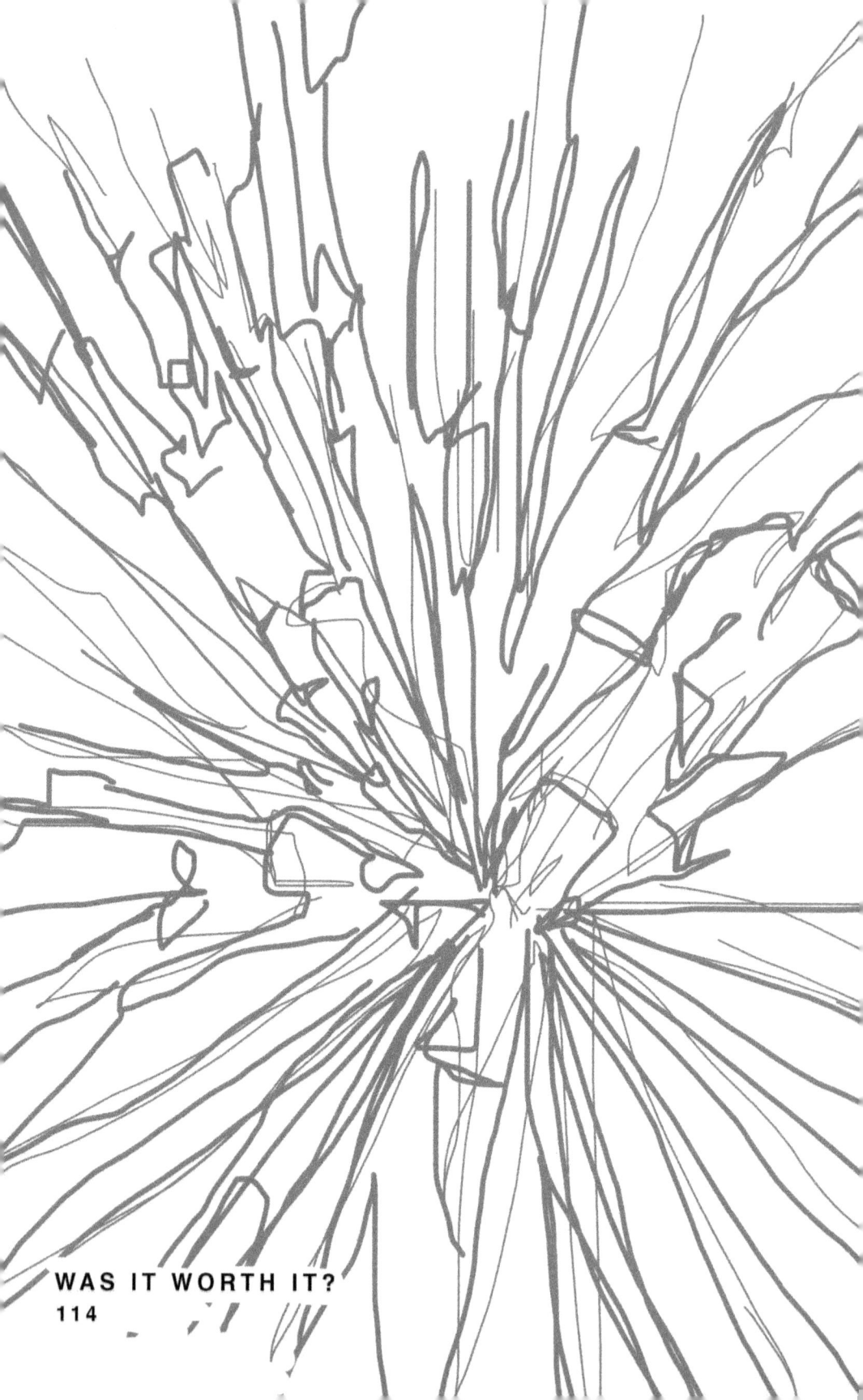

WAS IT WORTH IT?

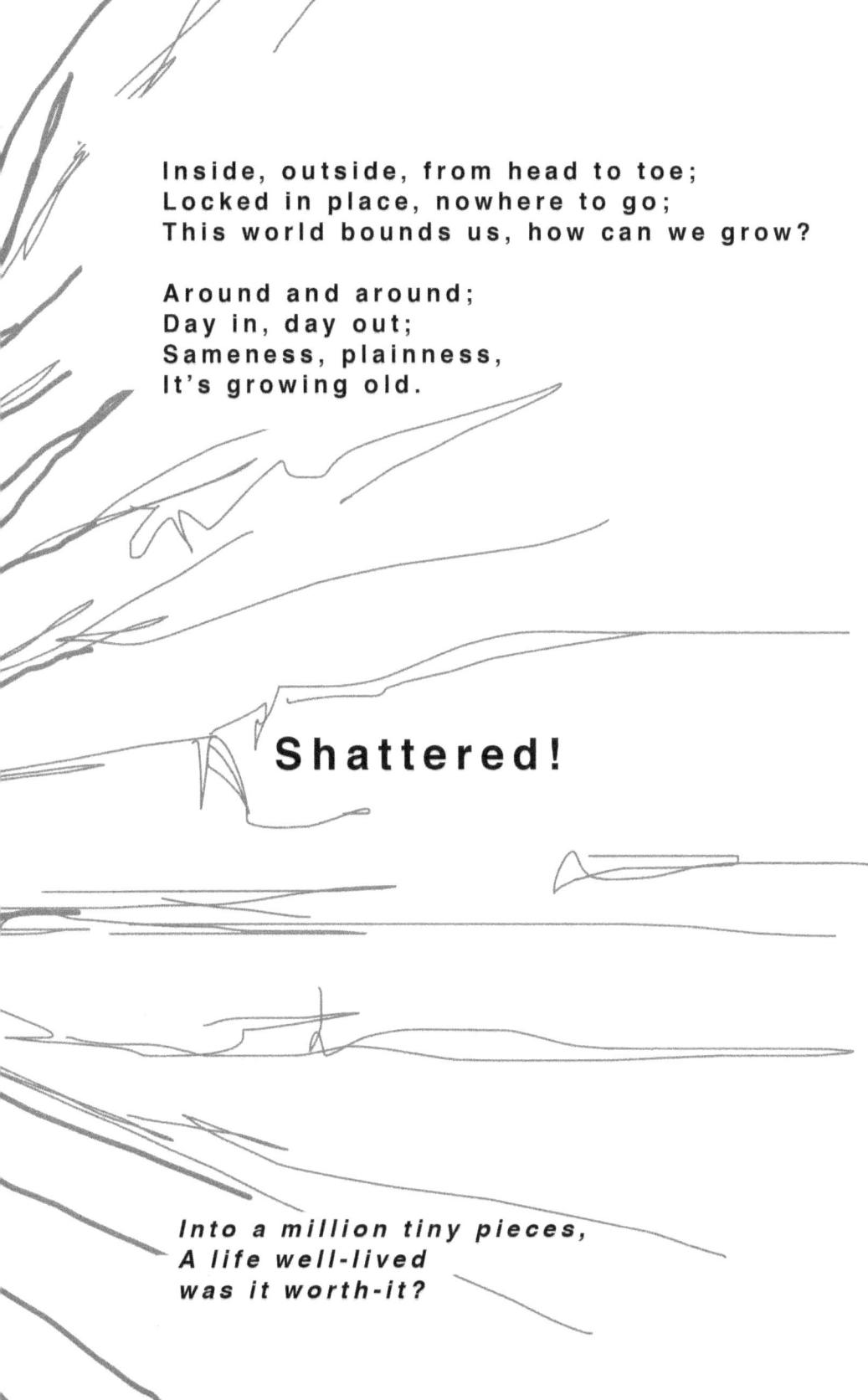

Inside, outside, from head to toe;
Locked in place, nowhere to go;
This world bounds us, how can we grow?

Around and around;
Day in, day out;
Sameness, plainness,
It's growing old.

Shattered!

Into a million tiny pieces,
A life well-lived
was it worth-it?

Destruction, production;
Work, sleep, wake, repeat.

Work, sleep, wake, get away;
Vacation at last, mind relaxed.
Relapsed; forgetful is it not?

God damn, reboot, start over!

Over this, over that;
Over everything at last.

Time, space, a new face;
Look, see, hear, no fear;
Here and there, everywhere.

Our past, it went so fast;
Quite a shadow that was cast.

In the present at last, at last;
Nothing like this forecast.

*Would the present last,
or be more of the past...*

Alien cast?

IN THE PAST

In the past;
Life moved fast.
This alien mask;
That was cast.

Stuck in a box
Where pain knocks.

Sitting behind a desk,
Staring at a blank screen.
Life did not feel clean,
Doing the office thing.

What a mess!

Suffering.
Chronic, sciatic;
From the lower back down the right leg;
Shooting waves of misery.

Owwwwww!
'Oww!'
Ow!

This path of mine
Seemed out of line.

It wasn't fine;
But, this life had become mine.

Stuck in a box
Where pain knocks.

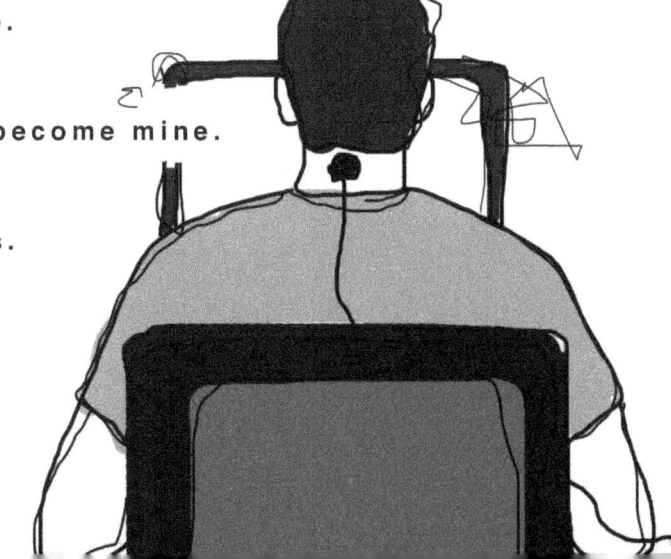

Under a roof;
Surrounded by walls;
Luminescent bulbs dulling all senses.

What have I become?
Better yet, what am I becoming?

These thoughts fluttered;
Flashed, popped.

Oh my!
My back, my leg.

'**Owwwwwww!**'

Stuck in a box;
Pain knocks.

Haunting yesterday;
Each day, every day.
Forgetting who we truly are.

At our core sits an essence;
Light, never fading...

Always there;
Deep inside simply waiting.

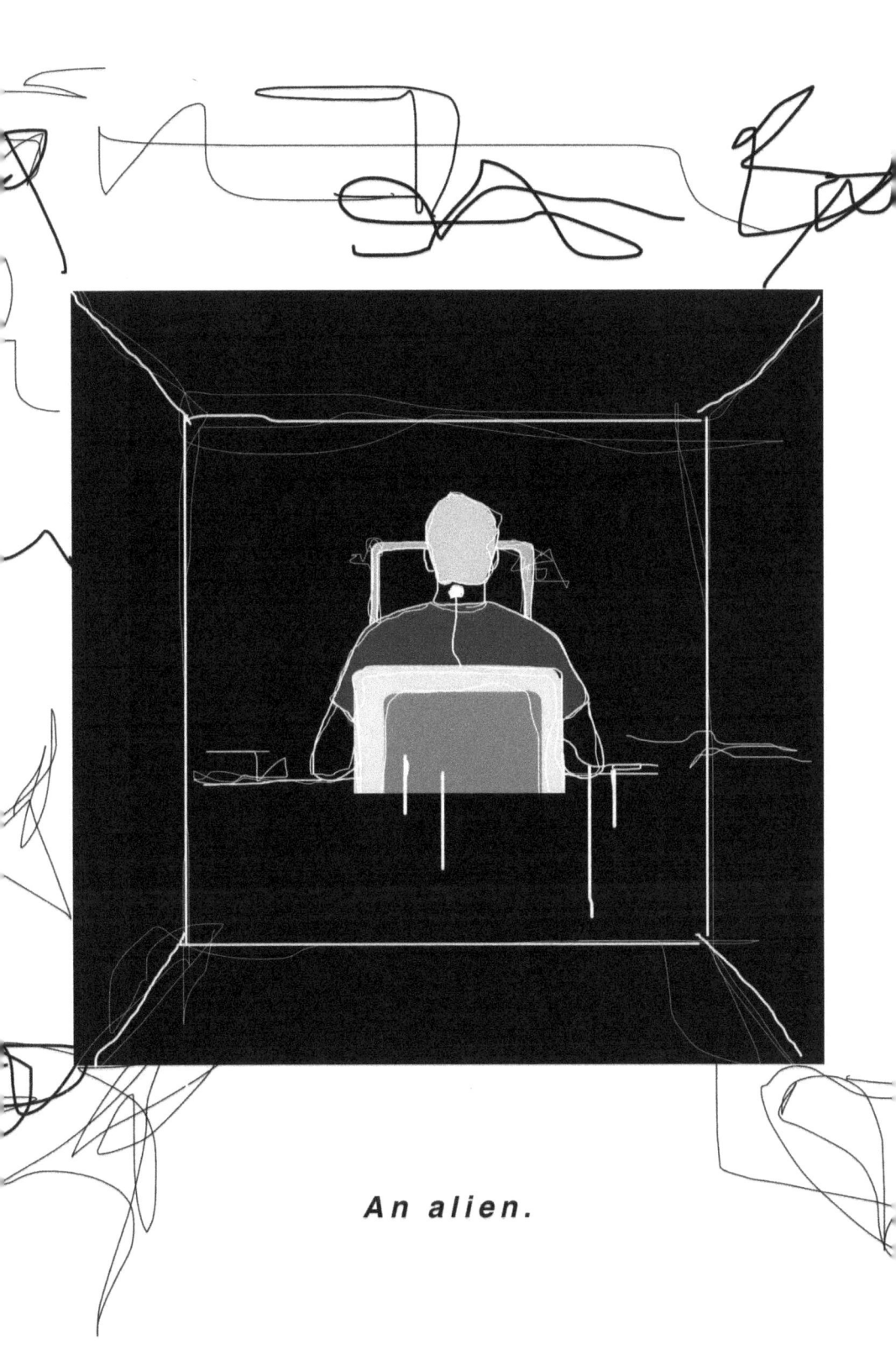

STUCK IN A BOX

This alien;
Stuck in a box
Where pain knocks.

Talks and talks;
Walks and walks;
Knock knock, **knock**.

Who's there?
It's me I swear.

I swear I swear, **'I swear!'**

Knocking on doors
Scaling floors;
From our cores
Out pours.

A new perspective
My detective;
So reflective
Introspective.

Ready to knock
To unlock a door;
Settle an old score
And find my roar.

Unlocking doors
To new shores;
From our cores
Using oars.

Discovering sand
This new land;
Again and again
Back to where it began.

Castaway
In alien gray;
Beyond the fray
Looking for something to say.

Hey!

Open up!

*Ready to knock
To unlock a door
Settle an old score
Find my roar;
And be an alien no more.*

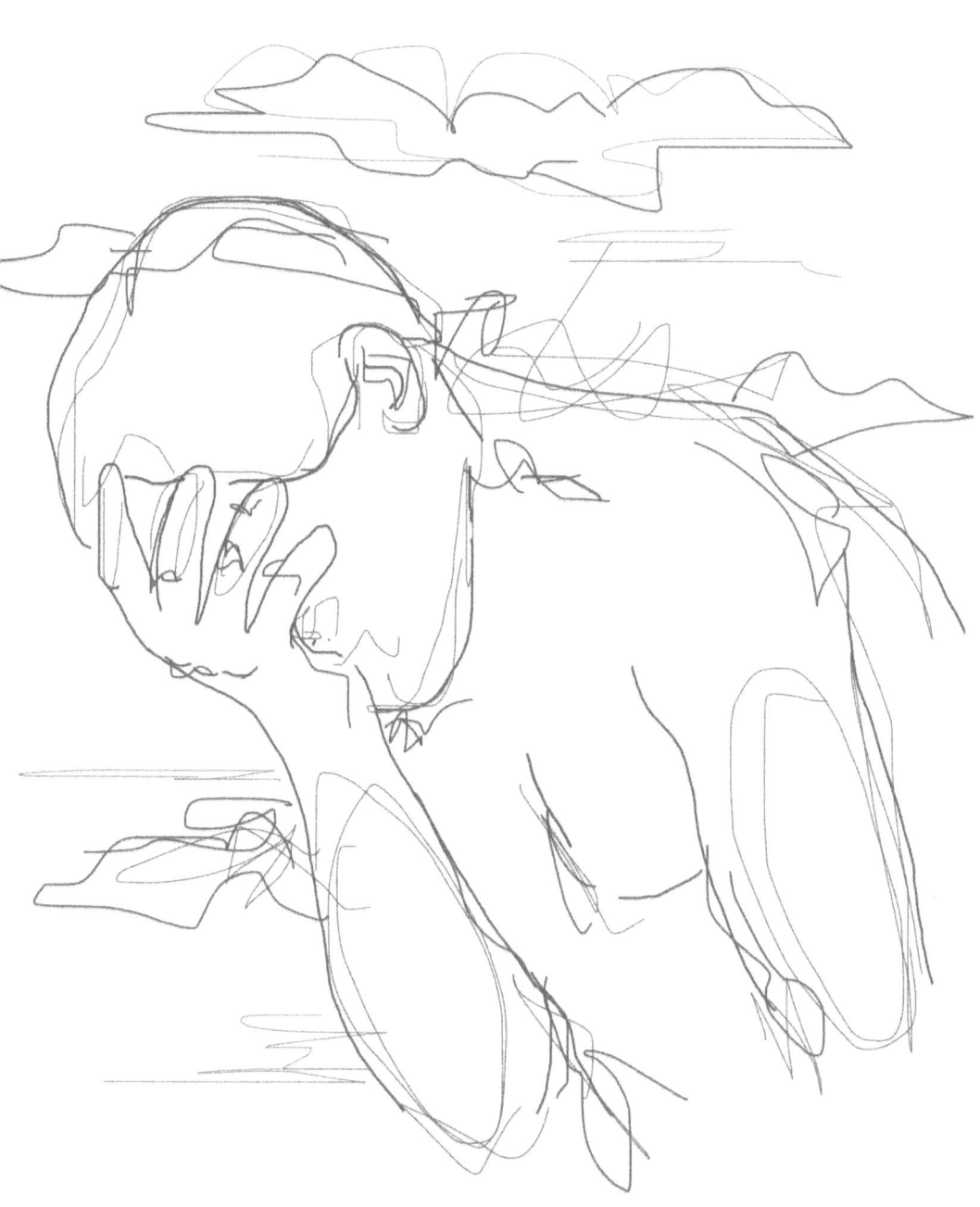

WAS IT ALL POINTLESS?

Or, I could go back to what I was doing before.
No roar.
No core.
An eyesore;
Far from shore.

When you have control of nothing;
When you let go of control.

How do you let go of something
You have worked for your whole life?

Was it all pointless?

If only, if only.

You could look back on all those regrets;
That's one thing I've realized.

I could regret all those things;
Or, I could appreciate...

I could appreciate what I've been given.

I've been given an opportunity
To have a free mind and a free will;
To live in a place where I can do that;
A lot of people don't get that privilege.

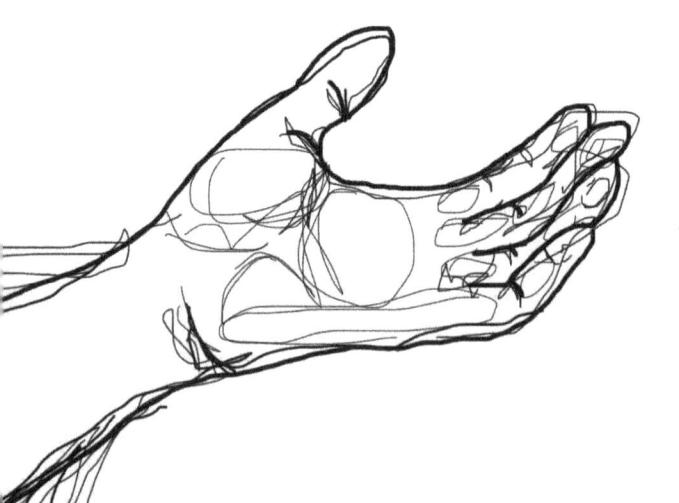

They don't.

That's real.

That's what a lot of people don't acknowledge.

They don't understand their privilege;
They don't recognize it;
They don't want to pay it forward;
They take it for their own;
It's selfish.

It was really selfish of me
For a long time.

I was selfish to myself;
And, I was selfish to others.

I was holding myself back from enjoying life;
Holding others back from enjoying
The warmth I could bring,
The glow that could surround me.

If only I could change my perspective.

If only I could let go.

It's hard to change your perspective
When you are stuck in somebody else's world.

An alien.

EVERYTHING BECOMES CLEAR

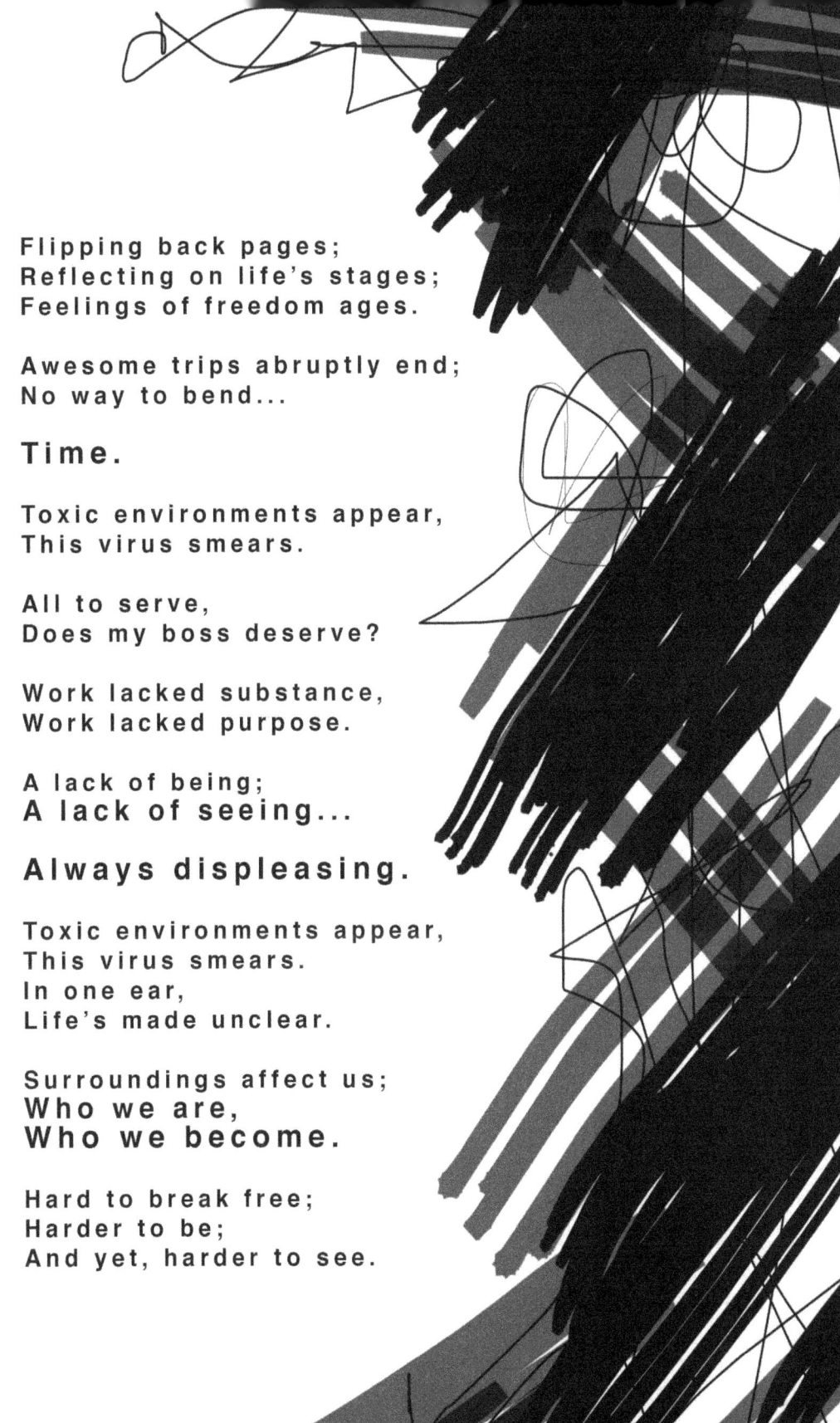

Flipping back pages;
Reflecting on life's stages;
Feelings of freedom ages.

Awesome trips abruptly end;
No way to bend...

Time.

Toxic environments appear,
This virus smears.

All to serve,
Does my boss deserve?

Work lacked substance,
Work lacked purpose.

A lack of being;
A lack of seeing...

Always displeasing.

Toxic environments appear,
This virus smears.
In one ear,
Life's made unclear.

Surroundings affect us;
Who we are,
Who we become.

Hard to break free;
Harder to be;
And yet, harder to see.

But, then we do.

We break free at last;
Enriching life, oh so fast.

Not taken for granted
Thoughts implanted.

Clarity long forgotten
Has been gotten.

Enveloped by calm.

Senses heightened;
Brain enlightened;
No longer frightened.

Toxic environments disappear,
As this virus clears.
In which we share,
Everything becomes clear.

Everything becomes clear.

Oh, wow!

Look at that,
It's beautiful!

*Toxic environments disappear,
Everything becomes clear.*

GRAVITY
134

Gravity pulled us in
Trapped us within
As we tried to swim.

Fearful demons won;
One by one.
Under an alien sun;
Nowhere to run.

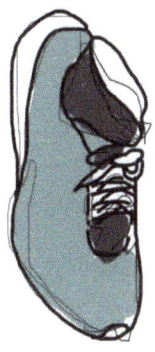
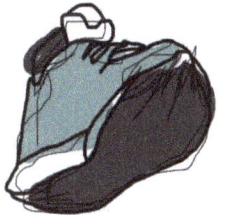

Until a hand, came from the land.

Until a hand came from the land.

Art, depart, a fresh start.

Hearing you, out of the blue;
Sending clue after clue,
Until I grew.

It helped me through,
Until my demons flew;
Now, my light shines true.

Gravity pulls me in
As I share this hymn;
Freed from within,
Where has this Earthling been?

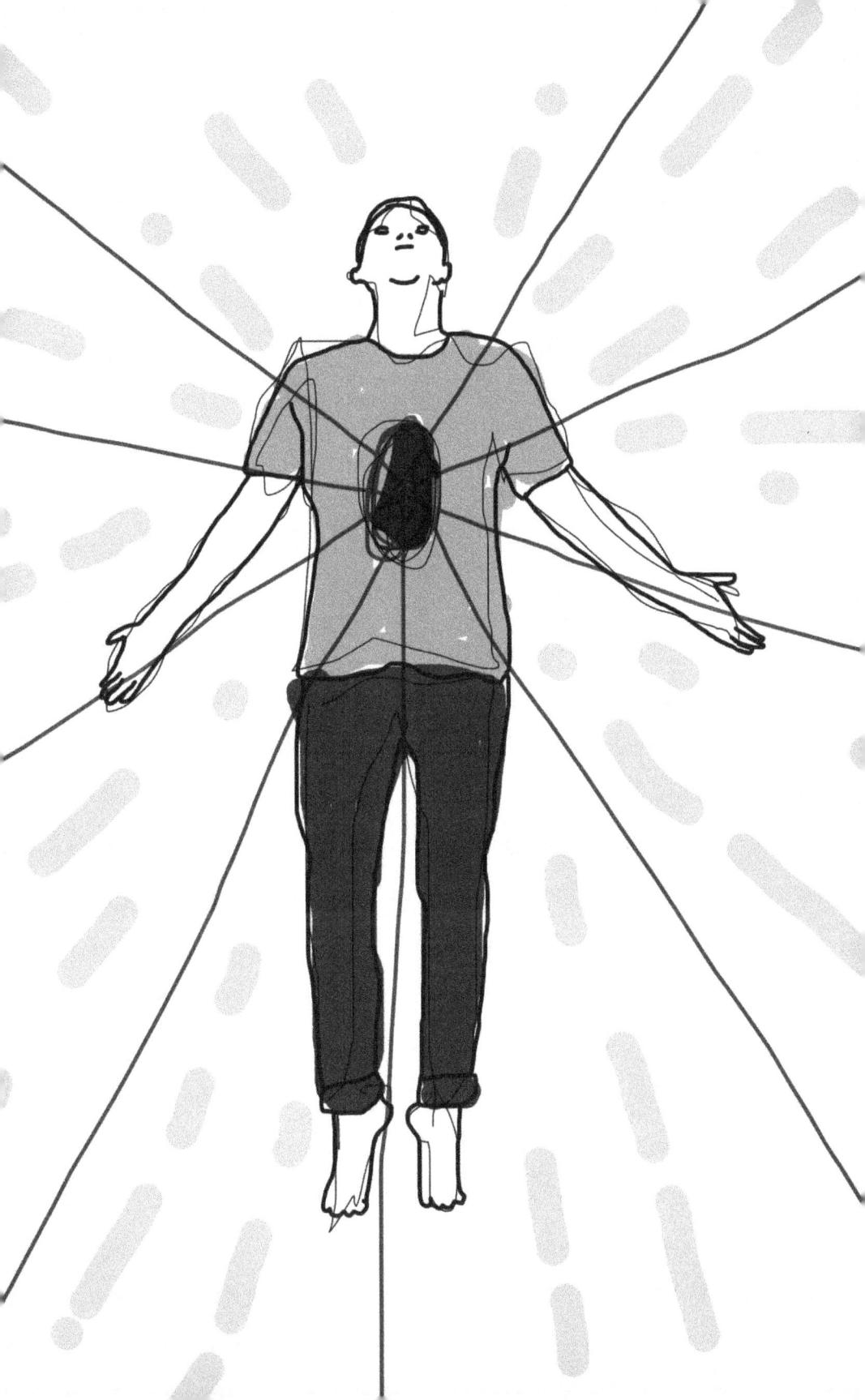

THE CONCRETE JUNGLE I ESCAPED

Like a coffin, trapped within,
The concrete jungle felt so thin.

Dead inside; Not alive.

A world flipped upside down;
Right side up is more like it.

No longer forced to park in a city
For a job I had grown to hate,
The concrete jungle I escaped.

Up the coast, into Redwood forests,
Freedom finally found;
Remembering what life is like when
distractions don't abound.

Sounds of birds, sounds of waves,
Sounds of nature every day.

A waking feeling to the joy of knowing
What you've found.

Cleansing minds of toxic waste,
Materialism had encased.

Drowning negativity for positive others have to give;
One step back, memories come flooding in,
Rushing through life rather than experiencing it,
tragedies begin.

Choices harder to make a time constraint,
No longer fun to live.

Escape or join the chase,
A choice I had to make.

One foot outside these invisible walls,
People trapped within.

It feels good to be free of this messed up state,
The concrete jungle I escaped.

It feels good to be free of this messed up state,
the concrete jungle I escaped.

Opening a new gate
To an awakened state;
Released from an alien fate;
This Earthling sits in wait.

WHAT'S NEXT?

With no expectations
Present at last;
My mind removed from its alien mask;
There are still questions people ask.

To which I say..,
Your guess is as good as mine.

Will it rain, will it shine;
It's fine, it's fine;
Was that a sign?

From line to line;
From time to time;
And, from rhyme to rhyme;
Your guess is as good as mine.

Whine, whine, say it ain't so,
Why is it that you don't know?

As with clouds above
The air in between,
What is seen in this scene?

Maybe, it's all just part of a dream.

Perspective, detective, conditioned to ask,
Questions that have come to pass.

Open up, shut up,
Life through a lens.

We see what we want, how we want,
When we want until our end.

It's what makes us
Unique, a geek, a freak,
Something we can seek.

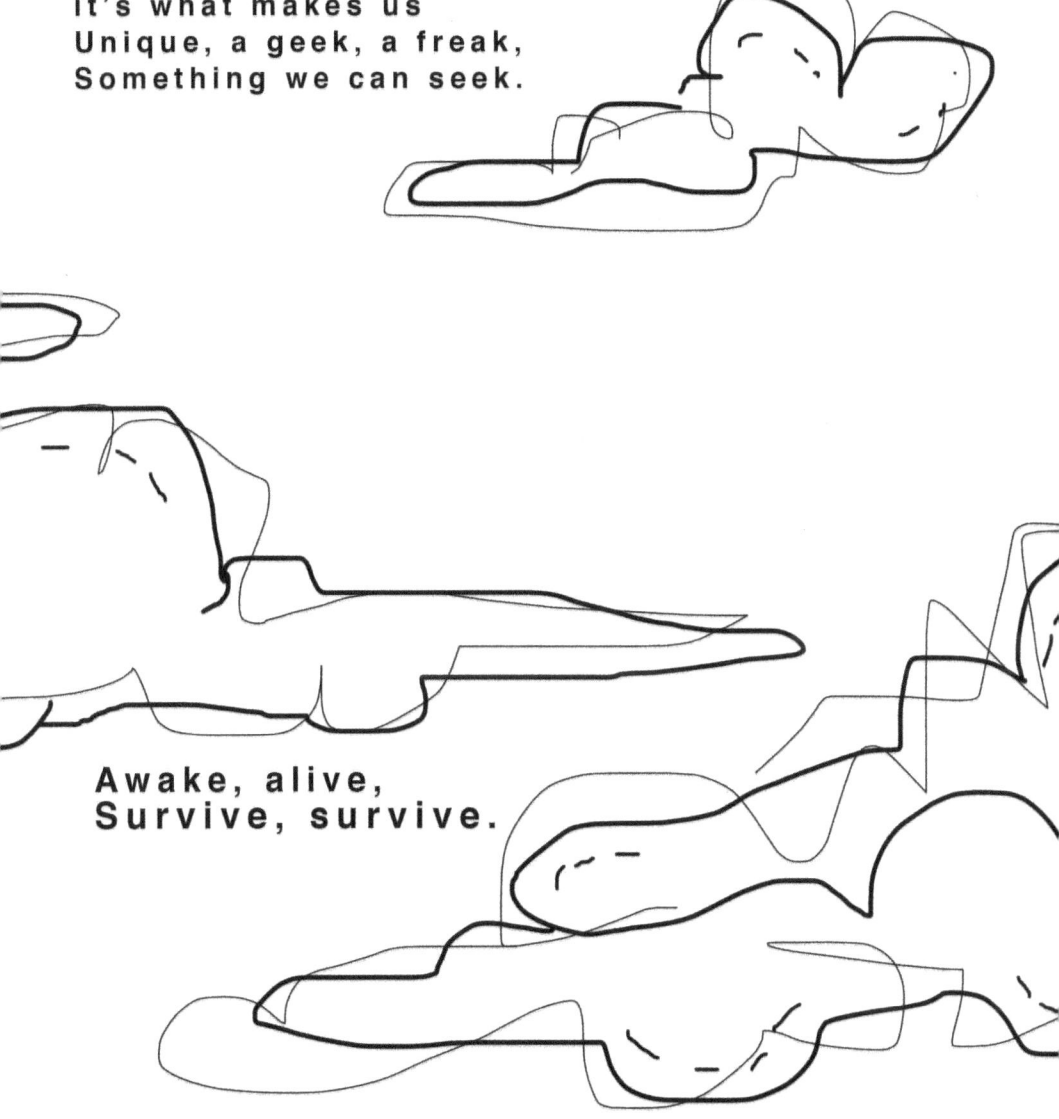

Awake, alive,
Survive, survive.

Gliding through space,
Outside the rat race;
New face, new pace,
Finding your place.

What's next, what's next,
What is next...

Today, tomorrow,
Each day after?

Your guess is as good as mine;
As good as mine, as good as mine,
Your guess is as good as mine.

This time like every time,
Your guess is as good as mine.

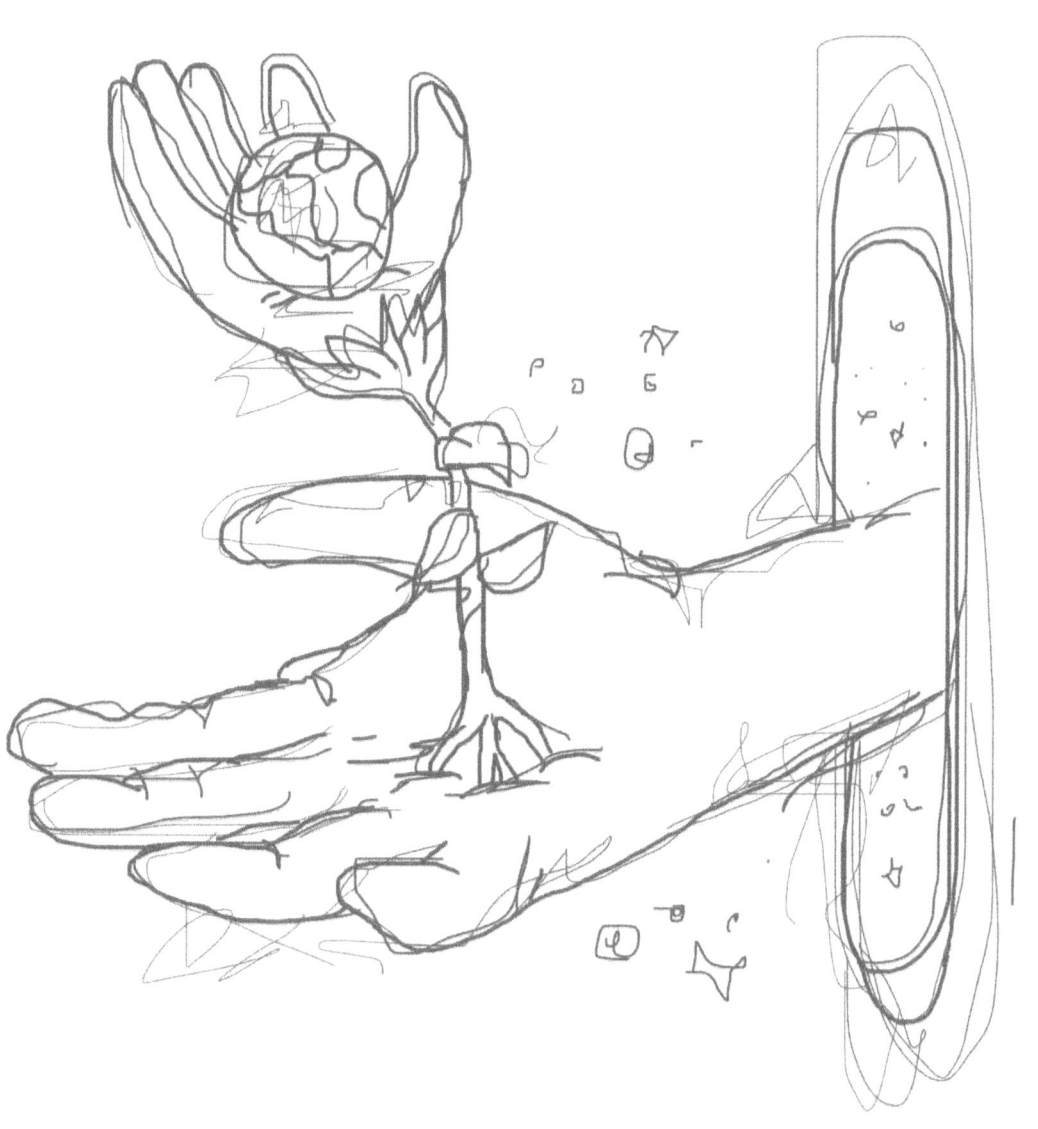

THE UNIVERSE KNOWS

What do you have to lose
When you follow the clues;
Why choose, why choose?

Nothing to lose
If you follow the clues.

Follow the clues.

Where the wind blows;
The universe knows
everything glows.

When everything glows
We break down lows.

We break down lows
When everything glows.

Who knows where one goes?
With this universal flow,
One goes
Where the wind blows.

That's how we grow,
In our reality show.
To gain universal flow,
Make everything glow.

All Earthlings know.

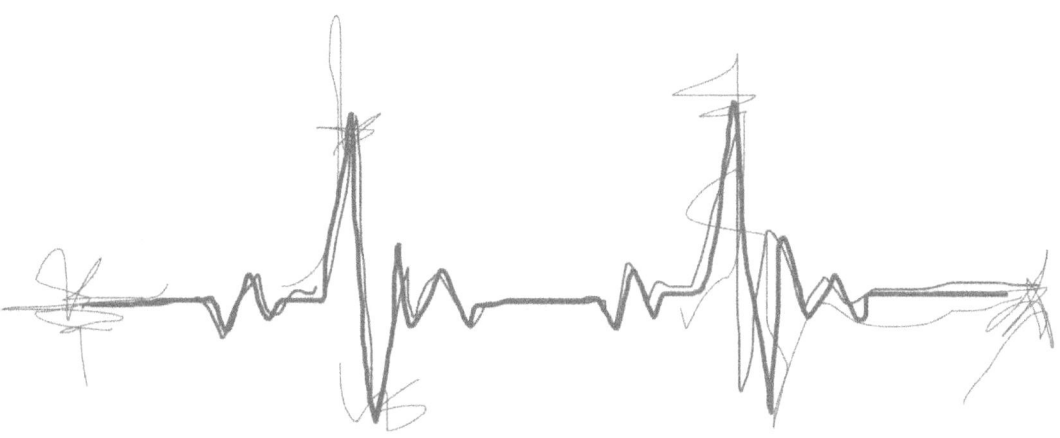

YOU ARE THE CATALYST, NOT I

You are the catalyst;
Someone told me.

Am I?

Not am I,
It doesn't matter.

What matters is that,
We're here together.

Brought together
Not by you or I, but by;
A common belief;
That when we're surrounded by community
Life becomes that much better.

Sharing is caring.
Caring is sharing.

The smiles;
The joy;
The pure jubilant laughter.

How does it get any better than that?

Smoky fire;
Flames to the sky;
Oh, how we all got so high.

High on life.

High on life.

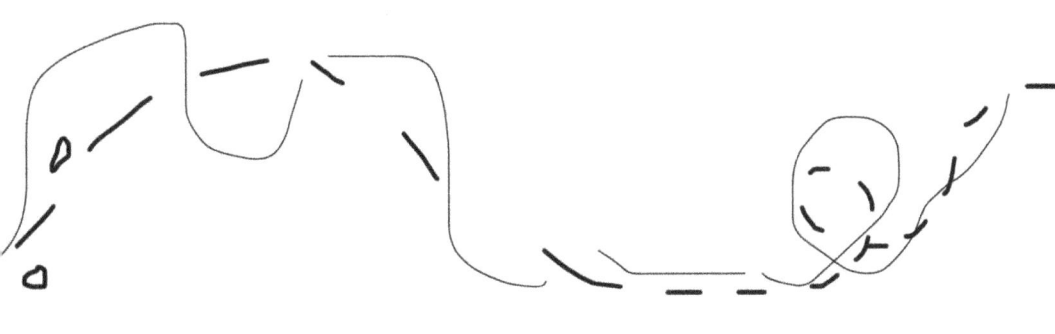

Above the clouds,
Beyond the sky,
Into the heavens we fly;
Oh, so high.

You are the catalyst, not I.

You are the catalyst, not I.

You are the catalyst, not I.

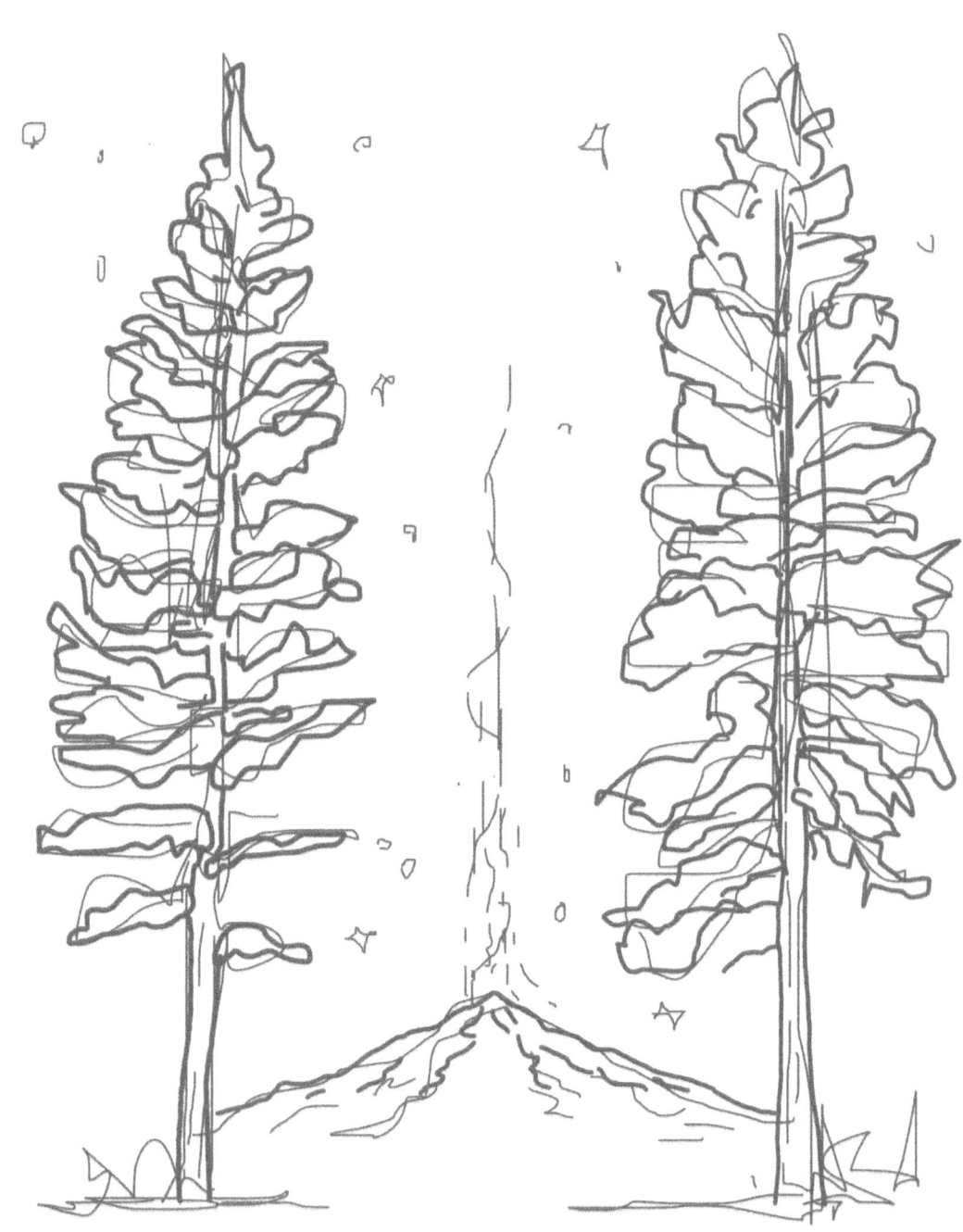

THANK YOU FOR BEING HERE

Sweet, sweet air,
My mind so clear;
Fresh mountain air,
Where I let go of fear.

Breaking down walls,
Bulldozing past falls;
Like waterfalls,
Nature calls.

River runs,
Under suns.
Crystal clear,
Nothing to fear.

Hiking up a long narrow path;
Through shadows the trees cast.

An endless seam,
Finding means,
Life feels clean.

Honest, true,
No sorrow, too.

**To do this, to do that,
To do it all, all,
All, at last.**

Let's move fast,
Shadows cast,
From this alien past.

Blast, blast, boom.

'Boom!'

'Zoom!'

Fresh mountain air,
My mind so clear;
Nothing to fear,
But being here.

Being here, being here,
PRESENT...

Present as can be,
Everyone can see;
So everyone can see,
And be present as can be.

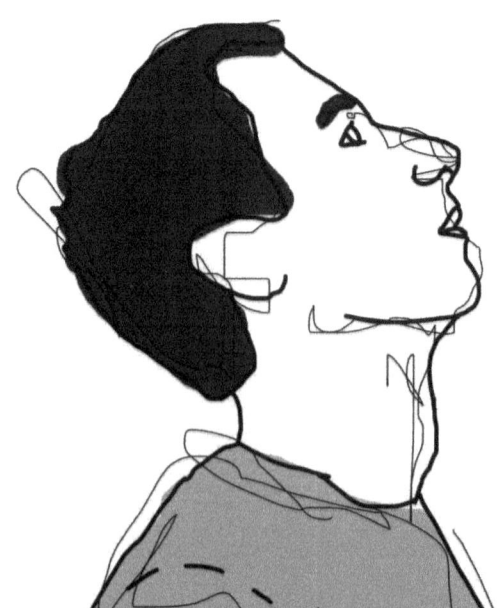

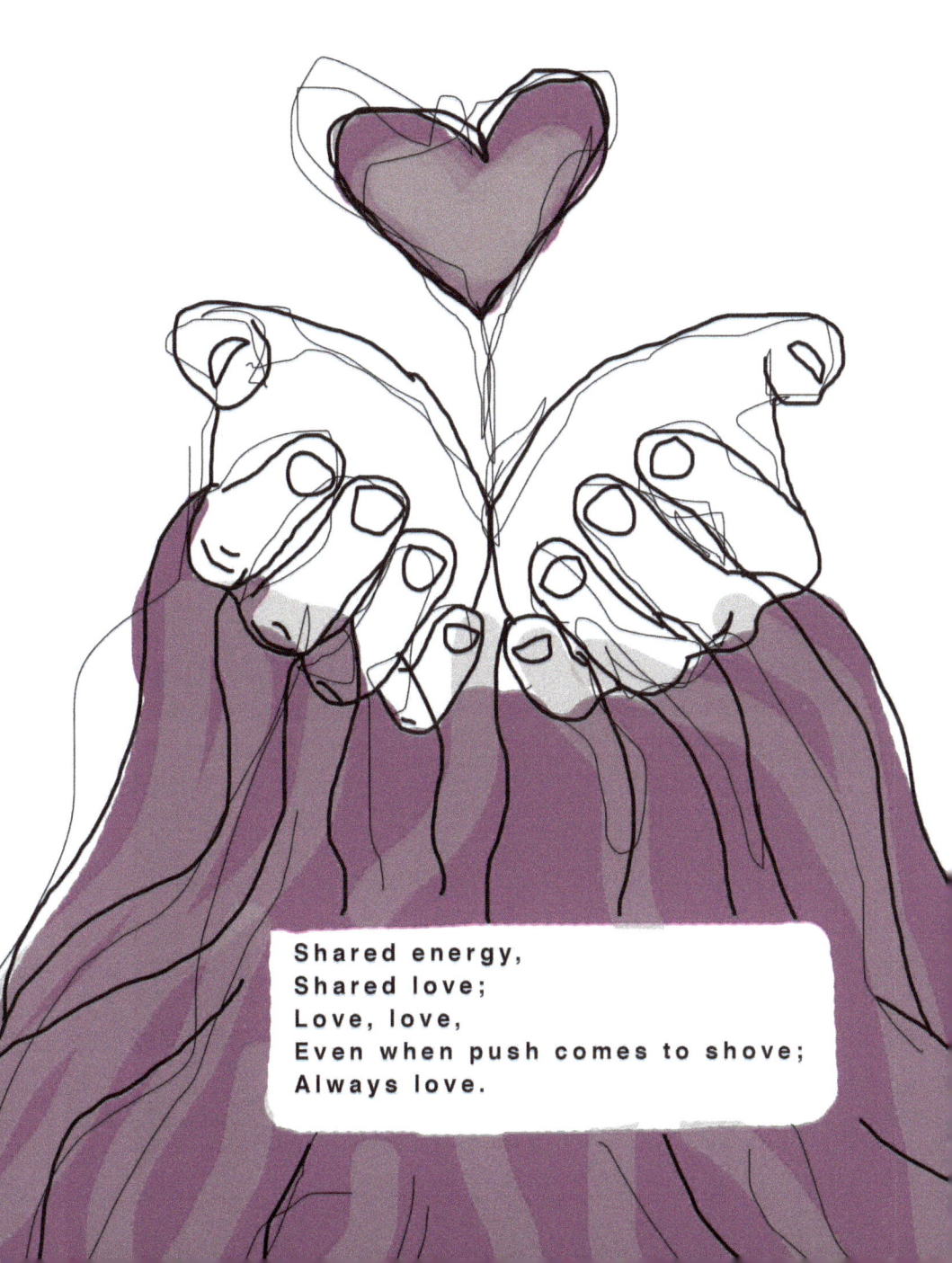

Running down this long narrow path;
Moving so fast,
Free of shadows that had been cast;
By my alien past.

Believe in your truth.
Only one,
Rising sun,
Let's have fun.

A new day,
To play away;
To which I say,
Thank you for being here.

Thank you for being here.

Thank you for being here.

Thank you for being here

Thank you for being here.

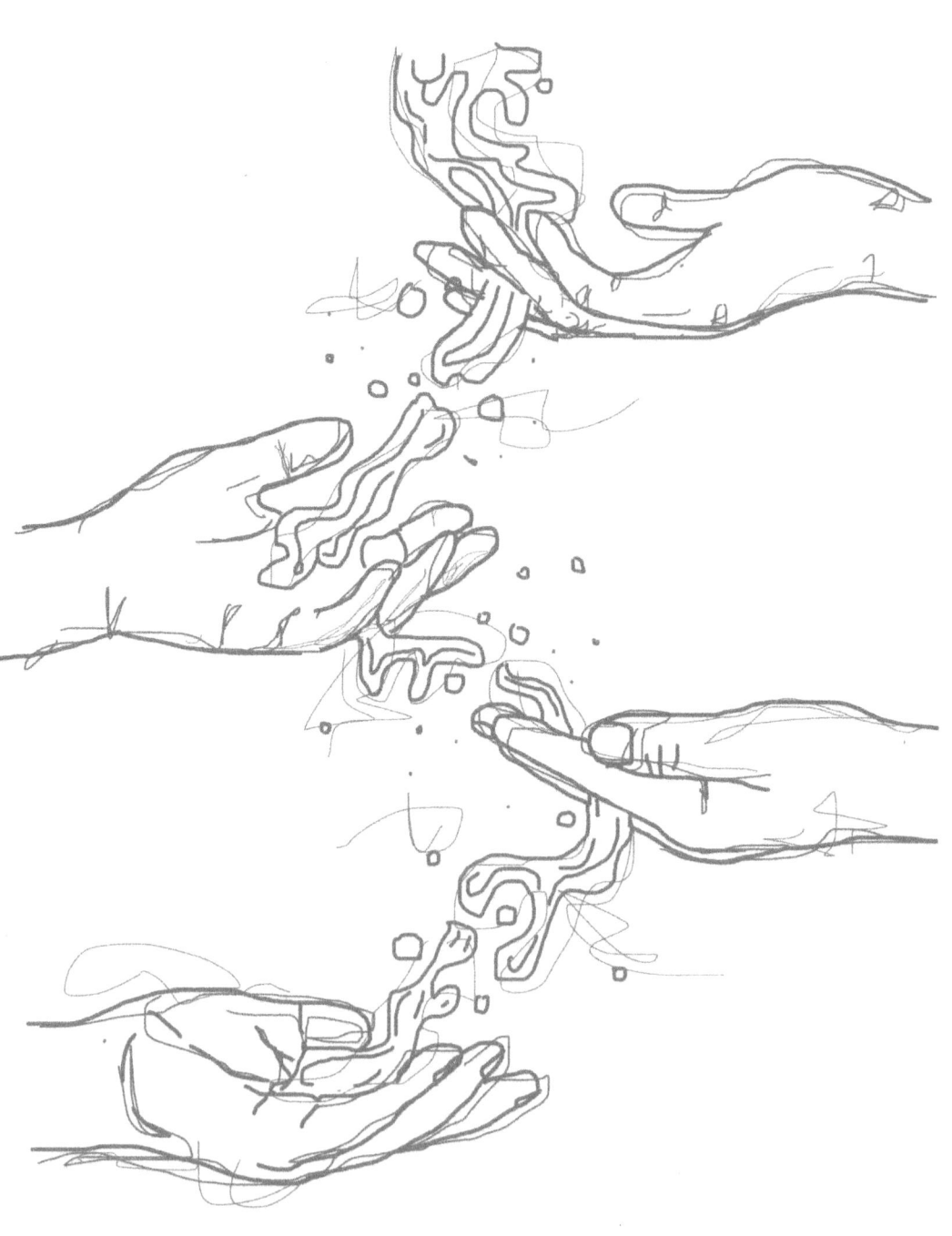

WHERE ARE YOU GOING?

Where are you from?
Where are you going?
How do you feel?

How we frame questions such as these
Subjects us to labels;
Perspectives, accurate or not.

People hoping to get a better understanding of us;
Rather than having to dig beneath the surface level,
Seeing our true spirit.

Currently, my destination is unknown;
To you, to me, as far as anyone can see.

From this planet, maybe;
Life, rife with possibility.

Reaching my full potential,
Which is exponential.

Each day, one at a time,
Trying to be present.

Some success, some failure.
Easy to say, **harder to do.**

Does this mean I'm lost?

Maybe, or It could be something much different.

My whole life prior to now
Feels more like a movie than reality.

A repeating scene the only dream.

Bad, good, low, high,
Happy, sad, even mad;
Emotions lifted from galaxies far far away.

Distant universes,
Memories fading from existence;
Yet, still a part of me.

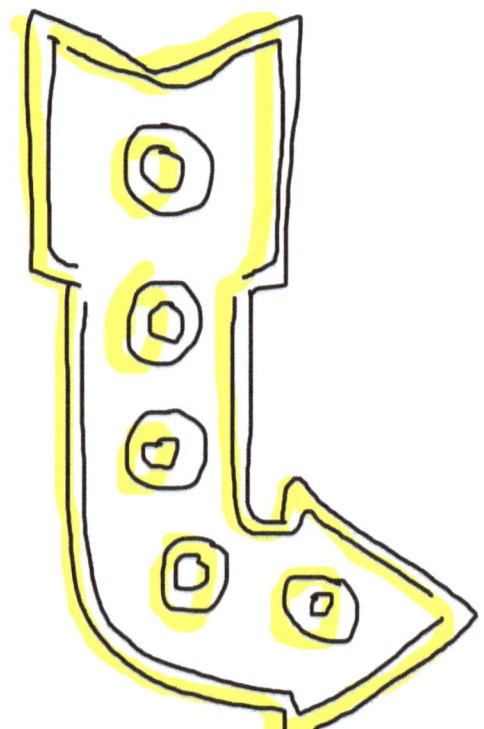

Am I running?
Am I hiding?

From what?

Discovering sounds more like it;
A soul lost until now.

An alien.

As far as I know,
The key to all this means letting go...

Of all labels;
Preconceptions;
Identity.

To connect with who we truly are;
Beneath the surface,
Lying dormant,
Waiting to come out.

Maybe, that's why over time,
It's lost waiting to be found.

My journey to nowhere has taken me everywhere.

At times feeling alone;
Confused,
Broken.

Searching for anything and everything.
Distracted from the here and now.

Seeking something yet to be foretold,
A dream waiting to unfold.

When I am asked,
"Where are you going?"
My destination is unknown.

What this life has shown;
Oh, how I've grown;
My destination is unknown.

My destination is unknown.

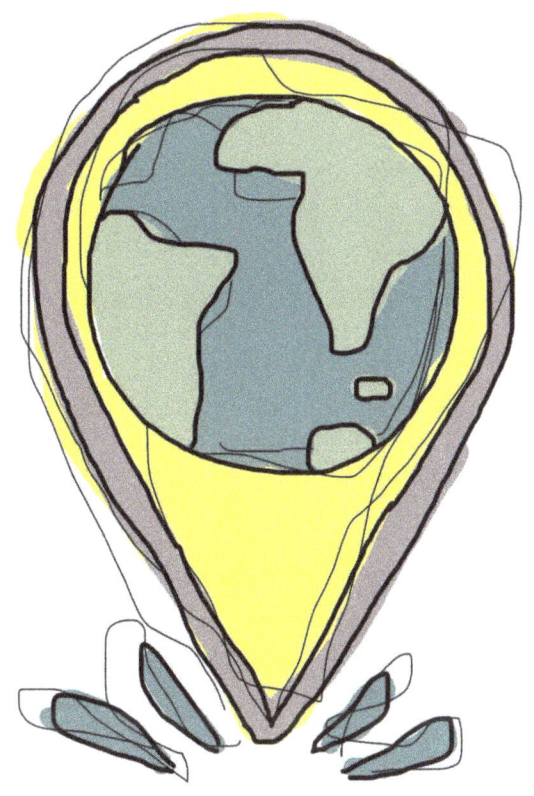

My destination is unknown.

What is known is that I've found home.

WHERE ARE YOU FROM?

Where are you from?

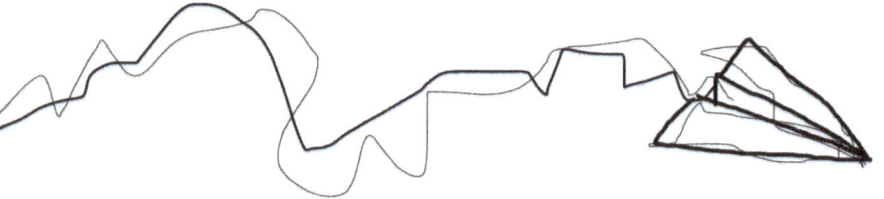

Earth.

People think I'm joking, but, It's the truth.

A universal home is more real to me,
Than anything else.

Growing up I always felt out of place.
No school or people,
No faith or group,
No culture or identity,
Gave me any sense of belonging.

Why close ourselves off to so much possibility?

Locked in a bubble,
Separating us from one reality to the next,
Belong or long for more.

I always dreamed and dreamed and dreamed,
From the outside looking in or so it seemed.

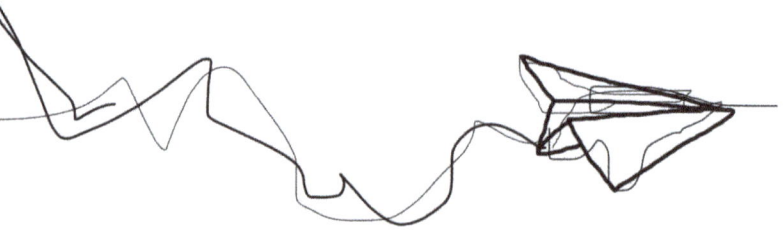

Maybe, I was really looking from the inside out.

I'm definitely not an alien,
However, it often feels that way.

Where are you from? Earth,
There's no place like home.

Realities come and go,
Life evolves,
Bubbles burst,
Change happens;
A universal truth.

Where I'm from doesn't matter;
Nor, where I am going;
For, right here, right now,
This is home as I like to call it.

This is home as I like to call it.

 This is home
      AS I LIKE TO CALL IT.

WHY DID YOU WRITE THIS?

Sick and tired,
Becoming wired,
On the path to being fired;
And then, rehired,
Instead, I retired.

We get stuck in loops.
Distracted from the here and now;
Unable to figure out how
To break the cycle.

My purpose in writing this book
Was to open my mind
So that everyone can find,
And I can remind;
That, we are not alone.

We are not alone.
We are in this together.

Our life is a journey,
Many lives in one.

Each day,
Each and every day;
No matter which way,
Within the fray;
Even when you are feeling gray,
Try to enjoy the day.

I wrote this book,
Because I was shook,
Told where to look,
Stuck in a nook.

Woken and spoken for, before,
All the time, my life was not mine,
The truest crime.

People showed me signs;
Natural rhymes and broken lines.

Not long ago,
I decided to forgo,
All that I know.

Here we go,
"I quit!"

My mind's been lit,
Now everything fits;
A past life blown into bits.

That's why I wrote this,
To share.

Now everyone can hear;
No matter where
You are, or how far,
Removed our scars;
Under stars
New signal bars,
Unleashed from jars.

Remember, you are not alone.

You are not alone.

INDEX

CHILDHOOD TRAUMA	6
SENSITIVE CREATURE	8
SEARCHING FOR HOME	16
WHERE AM I?	20
WHERE AM I FROM?	28
WHERE DID EVERYONE GO?	34
AM I ALONE?	40
IS THIS HOME?	46
HOW DO YOU FEEL?	52
ALIEN ME	56
NEVER FREE	60
DROWNING IN THE SEA	66
STILL SEARCHING FOR HOME	72
PURPOSE KNOWN	80
TO CHOOSE LOVE OVER FEAR	82
EVIL ACTS OF DESTRUCTION	88
THE WORLD REACTS	96
LIFE FREEZES	102
AN ALIEN ACT	106
TO BE HONEST	110
WAS IT WORTH IT?	114
IN THE PAST	118
STUCK IN A BOX	122
WAS IT ALL POINTLESS?	126
EVERYTHING BECOMES CLEAR	130
GRAVITY	134
THE CONCRETE JUNGLE I ESCAPED	138
WHAT IS NEXT	142
THE UNIVERSE KNOWS	148
YOU ARE THE CATALYST, NOT I	150
THANK YOU FOR BEING HERE	154
WHERE ARE YOU GOING?	160
WHERE ARE YOU FROM?	166
WHY I WROTE THIS	174

www.ingramcontent.com/pod-product-compliance
Lightning Source LLC
Chambersburg PA
CBHW061728070526
44583CB00024B/3049